Modern Masonry

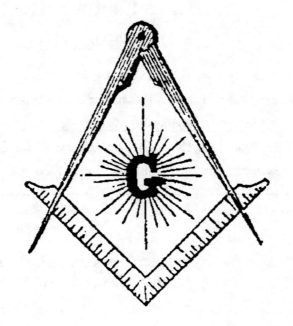

Joseph Fort Newton

ISBN 1-56459-043-7

8-96

PREFACE

THIS little book professes to be nothing more than the merest sketch and outline of the extraordinary development of Modern Masonry since the founding of the Grand Lodge of England in 1717. By its purpose it must be appraised, and by its record of facts it must be judged. It is no easy task to compress into so small a space so vast a stretch of time and so crowded a chronicle of events. Kept within the limits of a sketch, those etchings of personalities so interesting and illuminating to any narrative, have been left out, much to the regret of the writer.

Howbeit, such as it is it stands, and it is to be hoped that it will entice the reader to further explorations into the growth and spread of Masonry in the modern world. The Nile blessed old Egypt, whether the origin of it was the Mountains of the Moon, as some believed, or a Lake in central Africa, as we now know: so Masonry is to us a benediction, and some of us are as interested in whither it is going as whence it came.

—J. F. N.

TRESTLE-BOARD

MODERN MASONRY

===

CHAPTER I—THE BACKGROUND

I

MODERN MASONRY, in its origin and organization, is almost as much a mystery as ancient Masonry. It emerged suddenly out of dim and confused conditions, at the bidding of converging influences so intricate, and in a manner so extraordinary, that it is well nigh impossible to trace the process, much less to interpret it. Indeed, the impulse and urge which led to such a transformation are quite as obscure as the esoteric teaching which found fuller exposition and dramatization in its elaborated degrees. No doubt this is only what we should expect in the history of a secret fraternity, and we must accept the situation as we find it, drawing such inferences as the scattered facts and hints seem to justify.

Some one has recently pointed out, as a protest against the habit of those students who seek in the dark corners of history, among petty cults and obscure bands of handicraftsmen, for the origin of Masonry, that no one writing on the subject seems to have touched upon the fact, which ought to be open and obvious, that Masonry in its modern spirit and form is a child of the Reformation. The point is well taken,

1

and it is rather strange that it should have been over-looked, or at least not emphasized as it deserves, the more because it does give a key to an understanding of many things which otherwise remain dark.   At any rate it indicates the framework and environment in which the Craft developed, and why it allied itself so quickly and completely with the movement, or group of movements, in those nations and times in which the Reformation did its work most thoroughly.

During the Middle Ages, as we know, the Craft labored in the service of the Catholic Church, as the builder of cathedrals, abbeys, and other ecclesiastical establishments.   Its oldest documents, such as the Hal-liwell Manuscript—better known as the Regius Poem—dated about 1390, if not a priestly version of Charges still older, is such a document as a priest might have written, as its discoverer believed; invoking the Trinity and the Virgin Mary, and giving instructions for the proper observance of the Mass.   At that time, to be sure, as all through the Middle Ages, under the sur-face of conformity many cults, sects and movements, by the Church held to be heretical—the Patari, Cathari, Kabbalists, to name no others—were active and in-fluential; and they may have left deposits of their spirit and teaching in the rites and symbols of the Craft. Indeed, one has the feeling that there was something in the genius of the Craft which made it susceptible to such influences, and that these cultists and other forward-looking minds found in its rites and symbols a receptacle ready to receive the fermenting wine of those ideas which finally wrought the Reformation. Anyway, from the days of Edward VI on—or, say, by the time we reach the Harleian Ms. of the Old Charges, dated about 1600—a totally different influence and attitude are evident, showing that the Craft had cut its connection with Catholicism and had taken its place in the direct line of those forces which ultimately brought the freedom of the peoples, the liberty of conscience, the right of individual thought in religion, and the independence of manhood.

While, at the time of the Reformation, it is true to say that Masonry ceased to be Catholic and became Protestant in its affinities and affiliations, as well as in its faith and allegiance, it was still distinctively Christian in its teaching, and remained so for a long time afterward. Not until a much later time, and then only after struggle and schism, did it finally emancipate itself from any sectarian and dogmatic interpretation of Christianity, and attain its present independence with respect to the various religions, yet retaining a sympathetic appreciation of every elevating and benign form of the religious life; keeping, also, its own simple faith the while, and remaining essentially a religious institution. But that is a long story, a part of which it is the purpose of this record to recite, since it is necessary to an understanding of modern Masonry.

II

Against so long a background must we study the organization and development of Modern Masonry;

and it is evident, as we shall soon discover, that much else besides Operative Masonry went into the making of it. What we now call Speculative or Symbolical Masonry can be traced far back, just how far it is not possible to state exactly. Even the Regius Poem—earliest of records—in speaking of Prince Edwin of the tenth century, says, "Of speculatye he was a master"; with which agrees the Cook Ms., compiled in 1400 or earlier, which in referring to the same legend, uses these words: "lernyd practyke of yt sciens to his speculatyf. For of speculatyfe he was a Mastr and he lovyd well masonry and masons." Whether we accept the story of Prince Edwin as a fact does not matter; the record shows that the word "speculative" as applied to Masonry, as well as the idea, were both known and used. Of course it may be said that the Speculative referred to was the abstract theory of building, as distinct from the practical, or of philosophy in general. Still, as MacBride remarks, unless there was something else in Masonry than merely rules for operative workmen, we cannot understand the tale, if it be true, nor its invention if it be not true.

Just how far back the custom of admitting men who were not actual operative workmen as "Accepted" members of the Lodges began, is difficult to state definitely. The earliest reference to the fact that others than actual workmen were members of the Lodge is found in the minutes of the Lodge of Edinburgh, under date of June 8th, 1600; and it is not recorded as a thing unusual, but apparently customary—the names

of "Jhone Boiswell of Achinflek" and others being af-
fixed as witnesses of an initiation or entry. In 1652
Rev. James Ainslie was tried for being a Freemason
in his Diary telling of a visit to a Lodge in London
"that to their judgment there is neither sinne nor scan-
dale in that word (Mason's word) because in the
purest tymes of this kirke maisons haveing that word
have been ministers; that maisons haveing that word
have been, and are, daylie in our sessions, and many
professors haveing that word are daylie admitted to
the ordinances."

The famous entry in the Diary of Elias Ashmole,
under date of 1646, telling of his joining a lodge of
Freemasons at Warrington in Lancashire is a case in
point; and we now know that the Lodge was made
entirely of non-operative Masons. It seems plain, too,
that it was a speculative Lodge meeting temporarily at
Newcastle-on-Tyne, in which Sir Robert Moray was
initiated six years earlier. Ashmole has a second entry
in his Diary telling of a visit to a Lodge in London
in 1682, which met in Masons Hall. No doubt this is
the Lodge which Conder, the historian of the Mason's
Company, has traced back to 1620," and were the books
of the Company prior to that date in existence, we
should no doubt be able to trace the custom of re-
ceiving accepted members back to pre-Reformation
times." From an entry in the books of the Company,
dated 1665, it appears that "there was hanging up in
the Hall a list of the Accepted Masons enclosed in a'
faire frame, with a lock and key'."

Why was this? Conder asks; and answers it by saying that the Accepted Masons, or those who were initiated into the esoteric aspect of the Company, did not include the whole Company, and this was a list of the "enlightened ones," whose names were thus honored and kept on record, probably long after their decease. Then he adds: "This we cannot say for certain, but we can say that as early as 1620, and inferentially very much earlier, there were certain members of the Masons' Company and others who met from time to time to form a Lodge for the purpose of Speculative Masonry." He also mentions a copy of the Old Charges, or Gothic Constitutions, in the chest of the Masons' Company, known as "The Book of the Constitutions of the Accepted Masons."

Other such testimonies may be added. Of the forty-nine names on the roll of the Lodge of Aberdeen in 1670, thirty-nine were Accepted Masons in no way connected with the building trade. Randle Holme, the Chester antiquarian, was a member of a Lodge in 1665. Dr. Plot in a history of Staffordshire gives an account of Masons, their Old Charges, their use of signs, and speaks of them as spread more or less over the nation —under date of 1686. Aubrey, an antiquarian, made note of the Masons in 1691, saying that "they are known to one another by certain signs and watchwords, and that the manner of their adoption is very formal, with an oath of secrecy." Besides there are various references in the literature of the time—in the *Tatler*, for example—showing that Masonry was no longer a purely operative building craft, but had already become, largely, a speculative or symbolic fraternity long before what is called the "revival."

III

Just how "formal" the ceremonies of adoption were, to which Aubrey referred, we do not know. Some Lodges were made up entirely of operative Masons, others of Speculative Masons, and still others were of mixed membership. No doubt the ceremonies differed in different Lodges, and they would naturally tend to become more elaborate in purely speculative Lodges. Much of what in an operative Lodge was accepted as mere routine, or else as a task to be mastered in learning a trade, would, in a speculative Lodge, be exhibited as emblem or drama with moral or mystical suggestions. Hughan, Murray-Lyon, Hawkin, and others declare that there is no evidence in the old records of the Craft of more than one degree in the ancient operative Lodges, if indeed it can be called a degree at all in our sense of the word. They hold that the making of a Mason in the Craft Lodges was a very simple rite, consisting of the reading of an Old Charge and an oath, with, perhaps, some explanation of a symbol or two, nothing else. Such Degrees as the Fellowcraft and Master Mason, they insist, were not known and did not exist prior to 1777.

Gould, Speth, MacBride, and other students hold that there were at least two ceremonies, or degrees—or what we may fairly call the rudiments of degrees—in the old operative Lodges, though, of course, in much less elaborate form than we now know them. Both parties to the debate are, however, agreed that as far back as can be traced, there were three distinct grades of Masons, not necessarily degrees or ceremonies: Apprentice, Craftsmen, and Master. If this be so, there must have been some kind of formal distinction between them, as well as signs and tokens distinctive to each. A remarkable entry in the records of the Haughfoot Lodge, dated 1702, seems to indicate that there were two ceremonies, or at least two sets of grips and tokens. The first part of the minute is missing, having been written on a preceding page now lost. The remaining part is as follows:—"of entrie as the apprentice did leaving out (the Common Judge). Then they whisper the word as before, and the Master Mason grips his hand after the ordinary way." The "Common Judge" probably meant the "Common Gauge," and the record seems to imply more than one way of gripping, the ordinary way and some other way.

When we come to the Third Degree as we have it, which Anderson and Desaguliers were accused of fabricating, the case is more difficult, nor is this the time or place to go into the question. But two things are certain: first, the legend on which the degree is founded was known, in one form or another, long before; and second, no man or set of men could have invented a Degree made up of materials outside of, much less alien to, the traditions of the Craft, and foisted it upon the Lodges. If they made such a Degree, they did nothing more than fashion in ceremonial form what was well known to the Craft, otherwise they could never have introduced it; especially in Scotland, as MacBride points out, remembering the posture of the period and the qualities of the Scottish mind. "The Scottish mind was then full of the association of the Covenanters, and was not likely to view favorably any ritual coming from England."

Enough, then, for a swift sketch of the background of modern Masonry, as it slowly emerged from the gradually disappearing remains of the operative Craft. Those who regard Masonry as something more than a social club, or even a benevolent institution, are interested to the point of fascination in that period of dim half-light and much mystery out of which it arose. Knowing what Masonry is, naturally we have a keen curiosity to know how it came to be what it is. How much we should like to know about its development, how many questions we are ready to ask, answers to which are not found, or likely to be found, in fact, unless hitherto unguessed records should leap to light. Meantime the words of Woodford, uttered years ago, should describe our attitude:

"Where did the Freemasonry of 1717 come from? To accept for one moment the suggestion that so complex and curious a system, embracing so many archaic remains, and such skilfully adjusted ceremonies, so much connected matter accompanied by so many striking symbols, could have been the creation of a pious fraud or ingenious conviviality, presses heavily on our powers of belief and even passes over the normal credulity of our species. The traces of antiquity are too many to be overlooked or ignored."

CHAPTER II—THE "REVIVAL"

I

THE founding of the Grand Lodge of England in 1717 divided the history of Masonry into before and after. It not only gave a new date to our annals, but a new form and organization to Masonry, finding focus in the Grand Lodge, a new basis and spirit, and a new attitude both toward religion and politics—either one of which was enough to make it an epoch of far-reaching significance. It was more than a revival; it was a revolution. As some one has said, the date seems either a little too late or a little too early according to whether one means the acts which led up to the change or the process by which it found actual realization. None the less, as the result of ideas and forces organized at that time Masonry became the wondrous and widespread power which it is today and is destined to be in the future.

Yet, strangely enough, no movement of similar moment, one may venture to affirm, is so hidden from us, alike as to its facts and the influences which created it. What happened at the time of the so-called "revival," and in the period immediately following the founding of the Grand Lodge, is veiled in mystery and silence too deep to penetrate: nor do we know *why* it happened. The background is obscure, as we have discovered, and the records are too scanty and scrappy to enable us to trace the many influences which must have been at work culminating in the Constitutions of 1723, which, as Gould said, "may safely be ascribed to Anderson." Some of us would give much to know what lay behind and led up to that document, and to the Grand Lodge which adopted it, because, in any rightful reckoning, it must be accounted one of the great prophetic statements and platforms looking toward the unity and fraternity of man.

When describing "the great Masonic event of the eighteenth century, the Assembly of 1717," out of which sprang the Mother of Grand Lodges, Gould remarks that "unfortunately the minutes of Grand Lodge only commence on June 24th, 1723." For the history of the first six years of the new regime, therefore, we are mainly dependent on the account not written, or at least not published, until the second edition of the Constitutions in 1738—twenty-one years after the event to which it refers! Gould adds that nothing whatever relating to the proceedings of the Grand Lodge, except the "General Regulations" of 1721, was inserted in the earlier editions of the Constitutions in 1723; also, that no such thing as a "revival" was mentioned. It is quite useless to speculate why no minutes were kept, no record of any kind made of so important a gathering, or why it was organized without any Constitution; but perhaps it was only an experiment, in response to a growing need of a "center of Union and Harmony," and that those who took part in it did not dream that they were launching a movement destined to cover the earth with a great fraternal fellowship.

II

Taking the meager record as it has come down to us in the 1738 edition of the Constitutions, we learn that it was meant to be a revival of the Quarterly Communication. As to this Vibert very pertinently remarks: "It must be observed that there was nothing to revive on this occasion; and, in fact, in 1717 there is no doubt the fraternity adopted an organization of which no Mason or Lodge had any previous experience, or even tradition, except in so far as the Old Charges mention the Assembly; and even they contain no hint of a central governing body." Howbeit, the record as transmitted is as follows:

"King George I. entered London most magnificently on 20 September 1714. And after the Rebellion was over, 1716 A. D., the few Lodges at London, finding themselves neglected by Sir Christopher Wren, thought fit to cement under a Grand Master as the Center of Union and Harmony, viz., the Lodges that met:

(1) At the Goose and Gridiron Alehouse at St. Paul's Churchyard;

(2) At the Crown Alehouse in Parker's Lane, near Drury Lane;

(3) At the Apple Tree Tavern in Charles Street, Covent Garden;

(4) At the Rummer and Grapes Tavern in Channel Row, Westminster.

They and some old Brothers met at the said Apple Tree, and having put in the chair the oldest Master Mason (now the Master of a Lodge), they constituted themselves a Grand Lodge *pro tempore* in due form, and forthwith revived the Quarterly Communication of the officers of Lodges (Called the Grand Lodge), resolved to hold the annual assembly and Feast, and then to chuse a Grand Master from among themselves, till they should have the honor of a Noble Brother at their head."

"Accordingly on St. Baptist's Day, in the third year of King George I., 1717 A. D., the Assembly and Feast of the Free and Accepted Masons was held at the aforesaid Goose and Gridiron Alehouse."

"Before dinner, the oldest Master Mason (now the Master of a Lodge) in the chair, proposed a list of Candidates, and the Brethren, by a majority of hands, elected Mr. Anthony Sayer, gentleman, Grand Master of Masons—Capt. Joseph Elliot, Mr. Jacob Lamball, Carpenter, Grand Wardens—who being forthwith invested with the Badges of office and power, by the said oldest Master Mason, and installed, was duly congratulated and the assembly, who paid him the homage."

"Sayer Grand Master commanded the Masters and Wardens of Lodges to meet the Grand Officers every Quarter in Communication, at the place that he should appoint in his summons sent by the Tyler."

"N. B. It is called the Quarterly Communication, because it should meet Quarterly according to ancient usage. And when the Grand Master is present it is a Lodge in Ample Form; otherwise, only in Due Form, yet having the same authority with Ample Form."

Here, then, is the record, as it was published in 1738, of an event about which we know so little and would like to know so much. Whether this record was written at the time, or made at a later date in order to fill up the gap between the founding of the Grand Lodge and the opening of the minute book in June, 1723, we do not know. Anyway it is continued in the same brief, sketchy manner, and the chasm is bridged by a slight skeleton of scaffolding, if nothing more. Several interesting items appear betimes, as when Grand Master Payne, the following year, 1718, "desired any Brethren to bring to Grand Lodge any old writings and records concerning Masons and Masonry in order to shew the usages of ancient times: and this year several old copies of the Gothic Constitutions were produced and collated."

Again in 1720 we learn that "several very valuable Manuscripts (for they had nothing yet in print) concerning the Fraternity, their Lodges, Regulations, Charges, Secrets, and Usages (particularly one writ by Mr. Nicholas Stone the warden of Inigo Jones) were too hastily burnt by some scrupulous Brothers; that those papers might not fall into strange hands." Also it was agreed that "for the future the new Grand Master, as soon as he is installed, shall have the sole power of appointing both his Grand Wardens and a Deputy Grand Master (now found necessary as formerly) according to ancient custom, when Noble Brothers were Grand Masters." The following year a Noble Brother, John Duke of Montagu, became Grand

Master, to the great joy of the Craft, and the Grand Lodge moved to larger quarters in Stationers-Hall, Ludgate Street—security and prosperity having been achieved.

III

Diligent search among the records, diaries and newspapers of the day has enabled Hughan, Gould, Preston, Songhurst, Rylands, Crawley, Robbins and others to check, correct, and amplify some parts of the Anderson records; but it is still little more than a sketch, and it is doubtful if further facts will ever be forthcoming. While we are deeply in debt to Anderson, Preston, and Dermott, for such records as we have, none the less we must admit that they were often swayed by fancy and prejudice. They were well-meaning chroniclers, and devoted to the Craft, but each worked on his own theory of the events and of the power of the Grand Lodge—theories often very far apart. Unhappily, as we shall see, they did not always keep the peace among themselves, and as each was a special pleader for a set doctrine or policy, the discussions led to exaggerations and indiscretions.

Of "the few Lodges at London" who constituted themselves a Grand Lodge in due form in June, 1717, only four are named. If there were any other Lodges meeting in London at the time, it may be surmised that they had either not been notified of the purpose in mind or they had declined to associate themselves with the undertaking. The phrase "time immemorial," used to denote the date and age of the four Lodges is all a blur, telling us no authentic story of their origin and history. Howbeit, on the Engraved List of Lodges of 1729, the Goose and Gridiron Lodge No. 1, known afterward as the Lodge of Antiquity, is said to have dated from 1691, which may be the meeting referred to by Aubrey the antiquarian. Of the others we have no early knowledge at all, except their connection with the founding of the Grand Lodge. Even the Lodge of Antiquity pursued an uneventful career until Preston became its Master in 1774, when it was for a time involved in an angry dispute with Grand Lodge as to the inherent rights and authority of the original Lodges.

The Lodge meeting at the Crown, Parker's Lane— No. 2 of the original four—played no part in Masonic history, and died of inanition some twenty years later: stricken off the roll in 1740. No Mason of any note seems to have belonged to it. The Apple Tree Tavern Lodge—the original No. 3—gave to Grand Lodge its first Grand Master, Anthony Sayer, who, apparently, appointed two members of his own Lodge as Grand Wardens—so we may conjecture. The Lodge moved to the Queen's Head, Knave's Acre, about 1723, and there, if we may believe Anderson, "upon some difference, the members that met there came under a New Constitution, tho' they wanted it not"; referring, no doubt, to the Constitutions of the Grand Lodge adopted in that year. These three Lodges seem to have been operative Lodges, or largely so, composed of working Masons and Brethren of the artisan class, which may account for their lack of leadership.

The premier Lodge of the period which seems to have initiated and dictated the formation and policy of Grand Lodge was No. 4, meeting at the Rummer and Grape Tavern in Channel Row, Westminster. It was a Speculative Lodge, largely if not entirely, and all the leading men in the Craft in that formative time sprang from it. The other Lodges had perhaps twenty members each, while No. 4 had a roll of seventy, among them men of high social rank, such as the Duke of Richmond, Lord Paisley, Lord Waldegrave, Sir Richard Manningham, Count La Lippe, Baron des Kaw, Earl de Loraine, Marquis des Marches, William Cowper, Grand Secretary, and George Payne, Dr. Desaguliers, and James Anderson. This Lodge continued to hold first place in numbers, social rank, and influence until 1735, when a decline set in, both in attendance and contributions, and in 1747 it was decreed that the Lodge "be erased out of the Book of Lodges." Four years later the Lodge was restored, but it never regained its former prestige and prosperity, and twenty years later appeared to be once more on the verge of extinction, from which it was rescued by being merged with the Somerset House Lodge, founded by Dunckerley, who "exercised a positive genius in Masonic generalship."

From this first chapter of the Genesis of Modern Masonry, let us pass to a somewhat more detailed enquiry as to the nature and extent of the revolution wrought by the organization of the first Grand Lodge in 1717. The answer is that it was a complete and thorough-going revolution, as may be seen in the organization itself, in its General Regulations of 1721, and, later, in its Constitutions of 1723. Masonry was not simply revived, but refashioned, recast, and refounded on a different basis for a "more noble and glorious purpose," to use a tag from our recent Ritual. More specifically the details of the transformation may be outlined as follows:

First, the very idea of a Grand Lodge as a central governing body with supreme authority was novel, as much in its existence as in its extraordinary powers, unlike anything before known by the Craft. There had been certain old Lodges, to be sure, which had exercised some of the functions of a Grand Lodge, to the extent, at least, of giving authority and direction in the founding of other Lodges; as, for example, Mother Kilwinning Lodge, from which a series of Lodges were derived and established in various parts of Scotland; and these daughter Lodges added the name Kilwinning to their place name, so that we have Canongate Kilwinning, Torpichen Kilwinning, and so on. But the Grand Lodge of 1717 went further, in that it took complete command of its Lodges, even in matters of minute regulation—as in the offense for which Preston was expelled; and it is no wonder that this unheard-of authority provoked resentment and challenge, the more when it no longer confined its jurisdiction to Lodges "within ten miles of London," as at first declared, but invaded the Provinces.

Second, the office of Grand Master was new both in its creation and in the power with which it was invested; a power unquestioned, it would seem, from the first, and well nigh absolute—augmented apace until he had the "sole" power of appointing both his Wardens. The new power, as we read in the Anderson record, "now found as necessary as formerly, according to ancient custom, when Noble Brothers were Grand Masters," was an attempt to justify a new fact by appeal to an old fiction, since no such office existed in former times. Happily the early Grand Masters—with one notable and tragic exception—were wise men in no way disposed to exercise, much less abuse, the vast power with which they were invested; but that does not disguise the fact that the office was an innovation in the history and government of the Craft.

Third, it is pointed out by Gould that the Constitutions of 1723 introduced three other striking innovations, one of which was that it prohibited the working of the "Master's Part" in private Lodges, as if it intended to keep the most sacred and secret part of the Ritual within its own control, in the manner of the ancient Craft Assemblies. Such high-handed procedure provoked rebellion on the part of the Brethren, and was triumphantly swept away on November 27th, 1725. Further, it arbitrarily imposed upon the English Craft the use of two compound words—Entered Ap-

prentice and Fellow Craft—terms new in their ter-
minology. More serious still, the article on "God
and Religion" discarded Christianity as the only religion of Masonry; and Gould remarks, "the drawing
a sponge over the ancient Charge, 'to be true to God
and Holy Church,' was doubtless looked upon by many
Masons of those days in very much the same manner
as we now regard the absence of any religious formu-
lary whatever in the so-called Masonry of the Grand
Orient of France."

In short, as at the time of the Reformation the Craft
severed its connection with Catholicism, so in 1717
it severed itself from any one church, sect, or creed,
making itself henceforth independent of any school
of dogmatic theology. It proposed to unite men upon
the common eternal "religion in which all men agree,"
asking Masons to "keep their particular opinions to
themselves" and not make them tests of Masonic
fellowship. Oddly enough, the full import of this
article was not discovered, or at any rate was not made
an occasion of articulate dissension, until years later;
but in the middle of the century it was one factor leading to the organization of a rival Grand Lodge, and
a schism which lasted for fifty years.

V.

One other item deserves attention, not only to complete the list of innovations—if, indeed, it was an
innovation—but also to explain some very exciting
and high-colored happenings soon to transpire. To

what extent, if any, ancient Craft Masons mixed in politics is not easy to say exactly, though they were more than once suspected of such meddling, and their meetings interdicted. Whatever may have been true of old Craft Masonry, in nothing was the new Grand Lodge wiser than when, in its Constitutions, it "resolved against all Politics as what never yet conduced to the welfare of the Lodge, nor ever will." Indeed, at the very time when this law was being formulated by Grand Lodge, its wisdom was attested in a most dramatic manner by its own Grand Master, whose political activities made 1722-23 stormy years in the story of the Craft. Though not the Master of a Lodge, yet ambitious of the Chair, the Duke of Whorton got himself irregularly proclaimed Grand Master in June, 1722. To heal the "Breach of Harmony," the record tells us, the Duke of Montagu called Grand Lodge in session the following January, and had Whorton, who promised to be "True and Faithful," proclaimed Grand Master.

The origin of this astonishing affair, it soon became plain, was political rather than Masonic, it being the plan of the Duke of Whorton, who was a fanatical Jacobite, to use the power of the Craft against the House of Hanover, the reigning dynasty. Madcap and hot-spur, the Duke was not a man to do things by halves, and on the very day when Grand Lodge was assembling in June 1723, he was speaking in behalf of Jacobite candidates at Guildhall in the morning, while organizing for a struggle in the Grand

Lodge in the evening.' However, be it said to its credit, the Craft stood firm and refused to be dragged into the political arena, and adopted at that session the law just quoted. Failing to use the Fraternity in the interest of the Pretender, the Duke turned against it, trying to destroy it by ridicule, by concocting the fantastic caricature Order called the Gormogons, which ran its brief day, swallowed itself, and ended, accompanied by all kinds of exposures of Masonry.

Religion, too, Gould thinks, had something to do with this escapade, the wild Duke being used by influences in Rome, where the Pretender was then living. Not a few men of the Craft were opposed to the attitude of Grand Lodge toward religion, as too latitudinarian, equally obnoxious to the Roman Church and the High Church party in the Church of England. The Duke faded miserably out of both social and public life, dying five years later in Spain, a broken man, exiled for treason, and, despite many real gifts, mistrusted by all. Yet Count Goblet d'Alviella tells us that a tradition current in Belgium and in Spain represents Whorton as the founder of speculative Masonry in both countries. The Count is justified in asking, What created this reputation? His role as Grand Master seems hardly enough to warrant such a claim, if there is no other foundation to it. Truly it is an odd story, fit for romance, but its value to us is that it proves the wisdom of the Craft in avoiding political entanglements—a wisdom as valid today as in the past.

Surely it is an error to limit the Epoch of Transition, as it is called, to the first few years of Grand Lodge. It extended over a much longer period, say to 1735, or, rather, to 1738, when the new Book of Constitutions was published, and the first Papal Bull was launched against the Fraternity. It was a period of ups and downs, all kind of tangles, new and vexing issues, when the Craft was attacked and defended by turns, as we see from the items in the papers of the day which Sir Alfred Robbins has collected and collated in a fascinating essay, as well as in his study of Anderson and the Constitutions. Lodges multiplied, charity flourished and the Craft spread to many parts of the earth. In spite of dissensions within and opposition without, the Fraternity grew almost too rapidly, and measures had to be taken to restrain it. Even the Great Schism, which it is now my duty to report, helped rather than hindered the growth of Masonry.

CHAPTER III—THE GREAT SCHISM

I

THE Great Schism, which cut a cleavage in the Craft from 1751 to 1813, is very much of a puzzle. The explanations offered by our historians hardly explain it, least of all the motives lying behind it. Evidently the cement of Brotherly Love had not had time to harden, uniting the new, uprising Temple into one solid mass. Many elements were mixed, as usual, making the situation a medley not easy to analyze. Matters of rite, of race, of religion, of the authority of Grand Lodge and precedence among private Lodges, and the ever-present factor of personal ambition with which every society has to reckon, made complexity more complex. Such a state of things was amply conducive to division, if not to explosion, and the wonder is that the schisms were so few.

As early as 1730, and even earlier, complaints were heard of the "irregular" making of Masons, of which Grand Lodge took note. There was much carelessness in the matter: Lodges, and even private groups of Masons, made Masons with little regard for fitness and less for fees. Such practices tended to make Masonry cheap and ridiculous, its mysteries meaningless and its degrees jokes. So much so that Grand Lodge, in order to detect and, if possible check the evil, made slight changes in a few words in the early degrees; but to no avail. Instead of correcting the abuses the action of Grand Lodge only added irritation. It is plain, as Gould says, that the bonds of discipline urged by Grand Lodge were unequal, at first, to the burden which was imposed upon them, and the early Grand Masters stayed their hands until Grand Lodge "felt itself established on a sufficiently firm basis to be able to maintain in their integrity the General Regulations."

Other elements entered to complicate the problem. Not all of the Craft were willing to go as far as Grand Lodge went in the article on "God and Religion" in the Constitutions of 1723. Some time after 1738, and even before, we find Grand Lodge divided into two parties respecting this issue, one taking the Deistic side, and the other, claiming to be representatives of Ancient Masonry, taking the Christian side. As we have seen, the Apple Tree Lodge, one of the original Four, after some difference "came under a new constitution, tho' they wanted it not." Other Lodges were in similar mood, and it is significant that in the 1738 edition of the Constitutions the charge dealing with God and Religion, which in 1723 read: "In ancient times Masons were charged in every country to be of the religion of that Country or Nation," was altered and made to read: "In ancient times the *Christian* Masons were charged to comply with the *Christian* Usages of each Country where they travelled and worked." Howbeit, in the edition published in 1756 the original reading was restored and remained until 1815.

Here, then, are two causes of friction, as far apart as a flippant disregard of the sanctity of the degrees and the demand for a Christian explanation of its teaching. From the first, as we have seen, there was a tendency, due to the influence of some clergymen active in the order, as well as to many in the rank and mass, to give a distinctively Christian tinge to Masonry, both in its symbols and its ritual. This fact has not been enough emphasized by our historians, and it explains much. Yet of itself it would hardly have caused the Great Schism, but it did make an issue ready to hand when the Schism came, and it was used effectively. In 1738 for the first time Grand Lodge sanctioned an expansion of the Degrees—that is, the elaboration of the "Master's Part" into the Third Degree as we have it, which had been going on we know not how long—and this was deemed by many an "alteration of the established forms," and was made a further occasion for friction.

Let us not forget that the Craft suffered decline about this time, following the Papal Bull hurled at it. There were mock processions, and an organized campaign of buffoonery, with plenty of money behind it, intended, it would seem, to destroy the Fraternity by contempt and ridicule. In a letter to Horace Mann in 1743 Horace Walpole remarked that Masonry was in so low repute in England that nothing but a persecution could bring it back into vogue. Meantime, its old leaders were passing off the stage. Anderson died in 1739; Desaguliers in 1744. They were soon to be followed by other men of very different type and training—Preston and Dermott. one a journeyman-printer. the other a journeyman-painter. Sadler quietly remarks: "It would be quite possible to show from their own writings not merely a sufficiency but an affluence of proof that neither Dermott nor Preston was even superficially acquainted with the history of English Freemasonry between the years 1717 and 1751."

II

Still, so far, we have found no adequate explanation of the upheaval soon to rend the Craft asunder, making four, if not five, Grand Lodges instead of one, though the stage is plainly set for it. Gould in his large History, and again in his Concise edition, gives it as his ripe verdict, repeated with emphasis, that the summary erasure of Lodges from the list for not "paying in their charity," was one of the leading causes of the Secession. For this state of affairs he seems to blame Lord Byron, whose unpopularity was manifest, he argues, and who neglected the Craft during the five years he was Grand Master, 1747-52. If this be so, surely it is in order to ask why the Lodges did not pay in their charity, and this question he does not ask, much less answer. Whymper tries to exonerate Lord Byron, and if he is not entirely convincing, he does show that Gould was incorrect in his assertion that the schism was due to the erasure of Lodges.

Rather the erasure of Lodges was due to the discontent, and was an abortive effort to check it. Obviously we must go further back and deeper down to find the bottom, and it may be that Sadler was not far from the root of it when he suggested, if he did not prove, that the rival Grand Lodge was founded by Irish Masons settled in London. How strange, if true, that the Irish issue, an irritation in the world from a time to which the memory of man runneth not back to the contrary, was the secret of the great Schism in Freemasonry. Stranger things have happened, and it is a fact that a very strong Irish element was found in the membership of the new Masonic body, as well as in its leadership, and that its Constitutions and laws were fashioned after the Irish model. Anyway, as Calvert observes, the act of erasing Lodges from the list came too late; the stable door was locked after the horses had decamped.

The rival Grand Lodge was organized on February 5th, 1751, at the Griffin Tavern in Holborn, London, and the following year became known as "The Most Ancient and Honorable Fraternity of Free and Accepted Masons." It was a clever stroke of strategy, gathering up old grievances, adding up old irritations, and the older Grand Lodge was outwitted at every turn. Antiquity is dear to the hearts of Masons —the phrase "time immemorial," works like magic— and when the new body described itself as "Ancient," and its rival as "Modern," on the ground that the Grand Lodge of 1717 had abandoned the religious faith as well as the hoary rites and customs of the

Craft, it had an obvious advantage. At the outset the "Ancient" organization was governed by a Grand Committee—awaiting the time when it should have a Noble Brother for Grand Master—and the Committee, in its turn, was governed by Laurence Dermott, whom Calvert has described as "that most audacious, enthusiastic, vehement and indefatigable genius in the annals of Freemasonry, who was elected Grand Secretary in 1752 and remained the masterful organizer and guiding spirit of the schism for thirty-five years."

Dermott was an Irishman born in 1720, initiated in 1740, installed Master of Lodge No. 26 at Dublin in 1746, and in the same year became a Royal Arch Mason. He came to London as a journeyman painter in 1748, and soon afterwards joined a "Modern Lodge," from which he seceded to go with the "Ancients." Alert, wily, resourceful, not always scrupulous, a fighter with a gift of sarcasm, he left no stone unturned, no weapon unused, and the triumph of the movement was due largely to his efforts. Failing to find a Noble Brother for Grand Master, Robert Turner was elected in 1753. Three years later the Earl of Blessington came to the Chair, and during his reign of four years twenty Lodges were added to the roll, while a further sixty-four were added by 1766. By 1771, when the Duke of Atholl became Grand Master, with Dermott as his Deputy, the roll had reached the grand total of 197 Lodges under its warrants.

III

If, in this story, the religious issue has been emphasized, as an accompaniment, if not a cause, of the Schism, the reason becomes plain when we open the Book of Constitutions of the "Ancient" Grand Lodge, which appeared in 1756, under the fantastic title, *Ahiman Rezon;* published at his own risk, the Grand Secretary declared. It was derived from Ireland, and cast on the model of the Irish Constitutions, even the by-laws being a copy of the Irish by-laws. Under the first clause of Charges headed "Concerning God and Religion," we find the most emphatic recognition—nay, more, the affirmation—of Christian faith and teaching as the religion of Masonry. The article is as follows, the term "Noachida," referring to the belief that Masons are descended from Noah—an "ancient," indeed —who amidst the general impiety and depravity before the Flood, alone preserved the true knowledge and worship of God:

"A Mason is obliged by his tenure to observe the moral law as a true Noachida, and if he rightly understands the Craft, will never be a stupid Atheist, nor an irreligious Libertine, nor act against Conscience."

"In ancient Times, the Christian Masons were obliged to comply with the Christian usages of each Country where they travelled or worked, being found in all Nations, even of divers Religions."

Here is the article which Anderson inserted in the Constitutions of 1738, almost word for word; and the rest of the article is a close copy, or paraphrase, of the article of 1717, except the words, "they all agree in the three great Articles of Noah," whatever that may mean. Of course the implication of the whole controversy was that the original Grand Lodge was anti-Christian in its attitude, if not merely deistic in the vaguest kind of way. But that was not true, nor is it true of Masonry today, which is not anti-Christian, but it does refuse to make Christianity, in its sectarian and theological sense, a test of Masonic fellowship. As in the first Grand Lodge, so today, a man has a right to be a Christian in his faith, but he has no right to require another man to accept that faith in order to become a Mason. Faith in God, the Great Architect, is enough.

Returning to the "Ancient" Grand Lodge, we find in the ritual a confirmation of what is affirmed in the Constitution: it is all colored by distinctively Christian thought, imagery, and phraseology. For example, a prayer "to be said at the Opening of a Lodge or making of a Brother," includes these words: "Endow him with a Competency of Thy Divine Wisdom, that he may, with the secrets of Free-Masonry, be able to unfold the Mysteries of Godliness and Christianity. This we most humbly beg in the Name, and for the Sake, of Jesus Christ our Lord and Saviour. Amen." The following statement is conclusive, as much for its proof of the point, as for its thrust at the "Modern" Grand Lodge—whose Constitutions, by the way, contained no authorized prayers—as if

Atheism and Deism were on a par, whereas one denies God while the other believes in Him: "A Mason is obliged by his tenure to believe firmly in the true Worship of the eternal God, as well as in all those sacred Records which *the Dignitaries and Fathers of the Church have compiled* and published for the use of all good men: so that no one who rightly understands the Art, can possibly tread in the irreligious paths of the unhappy Libertine, or be induced to follow the arrogant Professors of Atheism or Deism." In short, the "Ancient" Grand Lodge was an orthodox trinitarian Christian body, and as such drew a line between Christian and Jewish Lodges.

IV

Nor was the "Ancient" Grand Lodge the only rival Grand Lodge to be recorded. The ancient city of York had long been a seat of the Masonic Craft, tradition tracing it back to the days of Athelsten in the tenth century. Whether the old society was a Private or a Grand Lodge is not plain; but on St. John the Evangelist's Day, 1725, it assumed the title of the "Grand Lodge of All England"—feeling no doubt, that its inherent right by virtue of antiquity had in some way been usurped by the advent of the Grand Lodge of London. After ten or fifteen years its minutes ceased, but in 1761 six of its surviving members revived the Grand Lodge, which continued with varying success until its final extinction in 1791, having only a few private Lodges, chiefly in Yorkshire.

Almost it seems as if the movement toward unity had been shattered, for we read of another Grand Lodge, called the Grand Lodge of England South of the River Trent, which grew out of a dispute between the Grand Lodge of London and the Lodge of Antiquity, of which Preston was Master, in 1779. It is not necessary to tell the story, except to say that Preston, by his ability and industry, had won a place among the "Moderns" not unlike that of Dermott among the "Ancients;" but his egotism carried him too far, causing him to defy Grand Lodge, as was then the habit, apparently, and set up, temporarily, a rival body under the authority of the Grand Lodge of York, or at least by alliance with it. Happily the breach was healed, and the Prestonian body with the two or three private Lodges which it had formed, returned to the fold. Still another body, calling itself "The Supreme Grand Lodge," has left faint traces of itself, as if trying to make up in name what it lacked in numbers; but its story is rather ghostly and not easy to track down to fact.

In spite of schism, perhaps because of it, Masonry grew, flourished and spread, amid a flood of attacks and exposures—some of them not only interesting but valuable to us. If our Brethren of those days did not obey the words of our later Ritual, to the effect that Masons are men among whom no contention should ever arise, save that noble contention, or rather emulation, as to who can best work and best agree, they none the less carried forward the great interests and enterprises of the Craft, equally in the industry of their propaganda and the munificence of their benevolence. If they sometimes lost sight of Brotherly Love and Truth in their wrangles—to say nothing of a too vivid imagination in their records—they did not forget the beautiful meaning of Relief. Each Grand Lodge watched the other, and what one did the other tried to outdo, but both were doing good work, and going in the right direction.

Rivalry stimulated enterprise. When the "Moderns" began to hold Lodges on board men-of-war, the "Ancients" cultivated the army, and by 1789 they had granted forty-nine warrants for Army Lodges, which carried Masonry into far places, both in the Old World and the New. Shakespeare Lodge started a fund for the founding of a School for Girls; whereupon the "Ancients" set up a School for Boys, intended to clothe and educate the sons of indigent Masons. While the "Moderns" were establishing Provincial Grand Lodges and cultivating friendly relations with France, the "Ancients" made alliance with the Grand Lodges of Scotland and Ireland. Both were busy in the New World, and thus was spun the network of influence and power destined to cover many lands.

CHAPTER IV—THE RECONCILIATION

I

AFTER all, what were the real differences in the dispute between the Grand Lodges in the Great Schism? At this distance it is difficult to decide, if we leave out the Irish influence as the root cause of the cleavage; and that is open to debate. None of the inciting causes alone, or even taken together, seems sufficient to justify such a breach of fellowship. The religious issue might have been settled, as is shown by the article and attitude in the Constitutions of 1738. In the actual or original Degrees of Masonry—the first three— there appears to have been no real, vital difference betwen the ceremonial of the rival fraternities. As some one put it aptly, there was no greater difference than there would be to dispute whether the glove should be placed on the right hand or the left.

Of course, the personal equation played a large part, but the struggle of ambitious men for leadership was not new in Masonry; nor, alas, is it novel today. When the last fact is found and the last word uttered, the matter remains a mystery, and will remain so to the end. While, as has been said, the schism was in many ways unhappy, it really made for the good of the Order in the sequel. The activity of rival Grand Lodges, always keen, often comic—as in the case of the Chevalier D'Eon, whose sex was a matter

35

of dispute and bet, until he himself had doubts, and in a fit of amazing aberration actually put on feminine habiliment[1]—and at times bitter, it promoted the spread of the principles of the Craft, to which all were alike loyal, as well as to the enrichment of its Ritual.

Dermott died in 1791, fighting to the end, implacable, uncompromising, unconquerable. More than once he had professed hope of a final union of the Grand Lodges, but he made no move toward it. Nor was there opportunity to do so. Even as late as April, 1777, the "Modern" Grand Lodge denounced the "Ancients" in severe terms, as irregular schismatics, due, apparently, to the fact that the rival body had increased so fast in numbers and power as almost to suggest that the "Moderns" were the offenders. However, not long after the death of Dermott the idea of a union of the two Grand Lodges began to be whispered about. With the passing away of old Brethren of both parties, a better mood made itself felt, and a desire to heal the feud grew, the way having

---

[1] Dermott was quick to see and seize this incident to make fun of his rivals, as we may read in a note in the edition of *Ahiman Rezon* for 1778, emphasizing the physical and sex qualifications of candidates for initiation:—"This is still the law of Ancient Masons though disregarded by our brethren (I mean sisters) the modern-masons, who, (some years ago) admitted Signiour Sing-Song, the Eunuch, T—nd—ci, at one of their Lodges in the Strand, London. And upon a late tryal at Westminster, it appeared that they had admitted a woman named Madam D'E—." Though legally declared to be a woman, it ought to be added that D'Eon was a man all the time, as was discovered at his death; but it was too good an opportunity for Dermott to miss to poke fun at his friendly foes.

been cleared, meanwhile, by the demise of the Grand Lodge of York. But the way of union was long and hard to travel, and the first step to that end was voted down in the Ancient Grand Lodge in 1797.

Again, in 1801-3, what Gould calls "the misdirected efforts of the Masonic authorities" well nigh made matters worse than ever, drawing from each Grand Lodge an invective against its rival. For six years no move was made on either side. In 1809, having made official alliance with Scotland and Ireland, the Modern Grand Lodge opened the door ajar by resolving that "it is not necessary any longer to continue in Force those measures which were resorted to, in or about the year 1739, respecting irregular Masons, and do therefore enjoin the several Lodges to revert to the Ancient Land Marks of the Society." To that end the Earl of Moira issued a warrant for a Lodge to be called "The Special Lodge of Promulgation" —a kind of go-between Lodge, so to speak—to study both systems and report. The report was to the effect that no great dissimilarity was found to exist between the "Ancient" and "Modern" systems, and where differences were detected the "Ancient" method seemed wise, as for example, the office of Deacon, up to that time unknown in "Modern" Lodges.

Slowly the door was opened a little wider, but the Brethren of the "Ancient" Grand Lodge were a little slow in their response—held back, for a time, by a Brother Harper, a jeweller in Fleet Street, who sold badges to the Lodges, and did not want business upset.

Happily, by 1810 committees were meeting and reporting on the "propriety and practicability of union," and a meeting of the two Grand Masters, the Earl of Moira and the Duke of Atholl, was arranged. Events moved rapidly toward the long-desired consummation; both sides were anxious "to put an end to diversity and establish the one true system, and ready to concur in any plan for investigating and ascertaining the genuine course, and when demonstrated to walk in it." As if to make the picture perfect, the Duke of Atholl retired in favor of the Duke of Kent and the Duke of Sussex took the Chair in the Modern Lodge—putting two Royal Brothers at the head of the two bodies.

II

Union came at last, in a great Lodge of Reconciliation held in Freemasons' Hall, London, on St. John's Day, December 27, 1813. It was a memorable and inspiring scene as the two Grand Lodges, so long estranged, filed into the Hall, so mixed as to be indistinguishable the one from the other. Both Grand Masters had seats of honor in the East on either side of the Throne, while the Act of Union was read and confirmed by the Assembly. When that was done the Duke of Kent, in an eloquent address, retired in favor of the Duke of Sussex, who was elected Grand Master of the United Grand Lodge, with Masonic honors—the Grand Installation day being fixed, appropriately, for St. George's Day. It was a fraternal hour, each side willing to sacrifice prejudice in behalf of principles held in common by all, and equally anxious to preserve the Landmarks of the Craft—the most significant fact, perhaps, being that the Ancient Masons had insisted that Masonry erase such distinctively Christian color as had crept into it and return to its first platform.

Thereafter it was only a matter of details, and with such a spirit no difficulty was found in fusing the two bodies into one solid mass, cemented by good will, which, we may well believe, will be enduring. There is no need to follow here minutely all the items of discussion and agreement in the Articles of Union and the new Book of Constitutions. But we must set down the article on "God and Religion" as follows: "Let a man's religion or mode of worship be what it may, he is not excluded from the Order provided he believes in the glorious architect of heaven and earth, and practice the sacred duties of morality." Surely that is broad enough, high enough; and we ought to join with it the famous proclamation issued by the Grand Master, the Duke of Sussex, from Kensington Palace, in 1842, declaring that Masonry is not identified with any one religion to the exclusion of others, and men in India who were otherwise eligible and could make a sincere profession of faith in one living God, be they Hindus or Mohammedans, might petition for membership in the Craft. Such in our own day is the spirit and practice of Masonic universality, and from that position, we may be very sure, the Craft will never recede.

One other Article of Union deserves attention, the second, as follows: "It is declared and pronounced that pure Ancient Masonry consists of three degrees, and no more; viz., those of the Entered Apprentice, the Fellow Craft, and the Master Mason (including the Supreme Order of the Holy Royal Arch)." The present sketch does not include a story of Capitular Masonry, which has its own history and historians, except to say that it seems to have begun about 1738-40, opinion differing as to whether it began in England or on the Continent. Dermott, always alert, had it adopted by the "Ancient" Grand Lodge about twenty-five years before the Grand Lodge of England took it up in 1770-76, when Thomas Dunckerley was appointed to arrange and introduce it: Dunckerley being one of many figures in those early years whose life was romantic, in origin and achievement, and who left "the best legacy he would have bequeathed to posterity"—an honorable name.

Quite rightly Dermott held the Royal Arch degree to be "the very essence of Masonry," albeit he was not slow in using it as a club with which to belabor the "Moderns"; but he did not originate it, as some have imagined, having received the degree before he came to London, perhaps in an early, undeveloped form. Even so Dunckerley was accused of shifting the original Grand Masonic Word from the Third Degree to the Royal Arch, and of substituting another in its stead. Enough to say the Royal Arch Degree—the other degrees that lead up to it in the American

Chapter are not officially recognized by the Grand Lodge of England even today, owing to the articles of Union, though they are tolerated separately—is authentic Masonry, being a further elaboration in drama and teaching of the spirit and *motif* of old Craft-Masonry.

As to the priority of Lodges, it was agreed at the Union that the oldest Lodges in each Grand Lodge should cast lots, and the winning Lodge becoming No. 1 on the list, the other No. 2, while the other Lodges were to fall in alternately. Unfortunately, the Lodge of Antiquity, one of the four original Lodges which constituted the first Grand Lodge in 1717, though actually the oldest, by bad luck won second place and became No. 2 on the new list. As many Lodges, under both systems, had ceased to exist, only 647 were actually carried forward at the Union, to which must be added the Grand Steward's Lodge which, by virtue of special privilege, was continued at the head of the list without number. With further details we need not now be detained, except to say that four years later, in 1817, the two Grand Chapters of the Royal Arch were united.

III

Two reflections may perhaps be allowed, as we turn from the story of the Lodge of Reconciliation, if only to underscore what must be in the mind of every reader. First, a regular Grand Lodge—the first, as all agree, ever formed—united with an irregular,

schismatic body, repeatedly denounced by it as irregular and illegitimate. It was not an absorption
but a Union on terms of equality, in all ways honorable to both sides—which makes one wonder what
we mean, historically, by legitimacy in Masonry.
Second, it is plain that the regular Grand Lodge made
all the advances for union, and pressed for it, over-
coming the reluctance of the rebel Grand Lodge. As
has been intimated, this urgency was due not only to
a desire for union, but to the fact that the rebel
Grand Lodge had grown to be so powerful as almost
to make the regular body seem irregular.

Yet, strangely enough, the older Grand Lodge actually won out on all the great issues involved in the
schism, the rebels yielding voluntarily, it would seem,
as if content to win on minor matters. The schismatics
surrendered on the religious issue, which had been
hotly contested, at least on their side of the dispute,
drawing the sponge, as Gould said, over the ancient
Charge "to be true to holy church," of their own ac-
cord and without protest. The older Grand Lodge
won out on "the expansion of the Degrees," about
which so much ado was made in 1739, and the three
degrees became the recognized ritual, with differences
only in detail. The regular Grand Lodge, in its turn,
had already recinded the irritating laws and changes
of words passed to detect irregularity, and it accepted
the office of Deacon as a valuable discovery. It was a
great feat of the genius of parley.

Once united, free of feud, cleansed of rancor, and

holding high its unsectarian, non-partisan flag, Masonry moved forward to its great ministry. If we would learn the lesson of those long-dead schisms, we must be vigilant and responsive to new days, correcting our judgments, improving our regulations, keeping the good of the Craft supreme; and above all cultivating the spirit of love which is the fountain whence issue all our voluntary efforts for what is right and true: union in essential matters, liberty in things unimportant and doubtful, Love always—one bond, one universal law, one cement against schism. Having traced the story thus far down the ways of time, we must now turn back, take up the threads, and trace the advance of Masonry in many ways and lands.

CHAPTER V—THE ADVANCE

I

TURNING back once more to the beginnings in the Epoch of Transition, 1717-1738, we find that the New Masonry had not only a new organization but a new impulse. From a few scattered Lodges —half operative, half speculative, and mixed—with no "center of union," and, apparently, with very little co-operation, it became a united and compact Fraternity. Whatever we may think of four Lodges forming a Grand Lodge, on their own initiative and by inherent right, and slowly but surely imposing their authority upon the rest of the Craft, it was abundantly justified by the results. It not only set the standard of Masonry, but it set a pace of organization and advance which carried the Craft, as we are now to learn, in an outward movement to the ends of the earth.

Of course we are handicapped, at first, by the absence or inaccuracy of records, and it still remains a mystery why the first Grand Lodge was organized without a Secretary and kept no minutes until June, 1724, when William Cowper became the first Grand Secretary. The Brethren of those days practiced the truly Masonic virtues of silence and circumspection, as much in the records as in their Ritual, both of which were in a tentative, formative stage. The authority of Grand Lodge may have been rather rigid at first, and relaxed too late to prevent rebellion and schism, yet one hardly sees how it could have been otherwise. The first "exposure" of Masonry by Samuel Pritchard, entitled *Masonry Dissected*—which Mackey says contained a "great deal of plausible matter, mingled with some truth as well as falsehood"—passed through many editions, and was quickly translated into French, German, and Dutch. It was followed by a counterblast under the title, *A Defence of Masonry*, by some ascribed to Anderson, and together they made a situation not easy to handle.

For a time it seemed as if Masonry, in spite of itself, was about to become public property; and this, with the riot of making Masons by wholesale and haphazard —by carelessly organized Lodges, and even by groups of Masons in private—called for stern measures, if the Craft was to be any longer a secret, much less a dignified, society. The Grand Lodge simply had to act, making a choice between the risk of rebellion and the more dangerous risk of chaos. It may not always have acted wisely in details, but it was compelled by the facts to act in a somewhat arbitrary manner, be the consequences what they might be. At first its jurisdiction was intended to be limited to Lodges in or near London, "within ten miles," to be more specific; but it soon went beyond those limits, and Lodges and groups of Lodges in the Provinces began, both voluntarily and by invitation, to come under its obedience; and the same reasons for having a central authority at all were equally valid in favor of extending it, whatever suspicion or jealousy or antagonism might be excited.

II

Consequently, as early as 1726, under the Grand Mastership of the Earl of Inchiquin, the practice of appointing Provincial Grand Masters began; and in May, 1727, we read in the Grand Minutes that Cowper, the Grand Marshal, was thanked by the Grand Lodge for his "visitation of the Lodges of Chester." Evidently it was a fruitful visitation, for about the same time a letter appears in the Minutes, signed by the Provincial Grand Master and his Officers, and addressed from the Castle and Falcon Lodge in Chester, proffering on behalf of "our whole fraternity our most cheerful obedience and extensive gratitude to our Superiours in London and Westminster." In June of the same year the Provincial Grand Master of South Wales returned thanks to the Grand Lodge, and in December the officers of the Lodge held at the King's Head in Salford, near Manchester, wrote to the Grand Master, "praying that the list of their members may be entered in the Grand Lodge Book," and that they be taken under his patronage and care.

Oddly enough, in 1728 a letter was received from a group of Masons at a Lodge in Madrid, in Spain, which had been constituted "sometime ago," they said, by the Duke of Whorton, asking to be entered on the Book of Lodges, and promising to forward "a longer List of Members," a copy of their laws, "and the Charity to the poor, so much recommended and exercised in Our Ancient Society." In response the Grand Lodge wrote to the Brethren in Spain assuring them—as they truly could, since the Lodge was founded by a former Grand Master—that they had been "acknowledged and received as Brethren." In November of the same year Charles Labelle, the Master of the Lodge of Madrid, was received in Grand Lodge, and the Minutes record that he "acquitted himself in a handsome manner like a Gentlemen and a good Mason." In these despites, we find the following entry in the Minutes under date of March 27th, 1729:—"The Master of the Lodge of Madrid stood up and represented that his Lodge had never been regularly constituted, and humbly prayed a Deputation for that purpose." Just what he meant is hard to say, unless he deemed the authority of "the mad, glad, sad, bad Duke" of Whorton inadequate. The Secretary was forthwith instructed to prepare the desired Deputation, and the importunate Master of Madrid drank the health of all present "and prosperity to the Craft wheresoever dispersed."

About the same time, 1728-29, warrants were granted by Grand Lodge for Lodges to be formed in places as far apart as Fort William in Bengal—probably the first of the purely military Lodges—Tunbridge Wells, Gibraltar, and Oxford. In June the following year, 1730, we read that the "Rt. Worshipful and well beloved Brother Daniel Cox of New Jersey Esqr"—so the record runs, as if New Jersey were an Esquire—was "nominated Ordained Constituted and appointed" Provincial Grand Master of the Provinces of New York, New Jersey and Pennsylvania by "His Grace the Duke of Norfolk"—then follow all the titles of the Duke, the last being—"Grand Master of the free and accepted Masons of England." It was the first appointment of a Provincial Grand Master for any part of the New World; but as Cox—also spelled Coxe—did not exercise his authority, and was not in America until after his Deputation had expired, he missed the honor of being the father and founder of regular Masonry in the New World.

For ten years after the founding of the Grand Lodge, it may be said in passing, no question of precedence among the Lodges appears to have been raised. Of course the original Four Lodges, as became their dignity, took priority. In the Minutes of December 19th. 1727, the Masters and Wardens of eighteen Lodges attended and answered to their names, but the Secretary, after placing the Four old Lodges at the head of the list, set the rest down without reference to the dates of their establishment. When the Minutes of that Communication had been read to the next Assembly, however, it was agreed to take up the matter of making more accurate lists in the order of the priority of the Lodges. Such lists of Lodges were required, of course, by the original Constitutions, "with the usual times and places of their forming and the names of all the members of each Lodge," as we read; but aside from giving the Four old Lodges the place of honor, no attempt seems to have been made to obey the Regulation literally in the matter of priority. Not until November, 1728, were the names of the several Lodges read over "according to their priority."

III

As we are now to follow Masonry out of England into other lands, it is well to remember that, like all other institutions, it has been modified by and adapted to the environment in which it has labored. While its principles and purpose are everywhere essentially the same, inevitably it has been influenced by the temperaments of different peoples, as well as by the uses to which it has been put. Vibert observes that "Masonry seems to be a plant that can only retain its true characteristics in British or Anglo-Saxon ground." Yet even in the British Isles Masonry seems somewhat different—in the temper, tone, and "feel" of it—in different places. Masonry in Scotland, for example, is more independent, more democratic, and less rigidly formal than it is in England, as any one can testify who has sat in Lodges in the two countries.

When we cross the Channel to the Continent we find even greater differences, as great as the differences in culture and moral code between the races. Even in Northern Europe the Craft has followed a different path of development, so that its working in Sweden is now distinct, if not alien, from our Masonry. In Latin countries the gap is still wider, made so as much by diversity of development and divergence of temperament as by the very different uses to which Masonry has been put, especially in France and Italy, where it has been in conflict with Governments as well as with the Latin Church. With these matters we shall deal later as they deserve and so far as the dimensions of this study will permit. Meantime, it will be more con-venient to trace the spread of Masonry geographically rather than chronologically, as the dates are not far apart, beginning with the British Isles and confining attention to Masonry as derived from or sanctioned by the Grand Lodge of England.

The actual records of a number of Lodges in Scot-land go much further back than any Lodge known in England. Indeed, so many Lodges in Scotland claim to be the oldest that it was for a long time a puzzle as to precedence, until a Masonic lawyer—he must have been of Irish origin—suggested that the question be settled by having more than one No. 1. Thus we find, in addition to Kilwinning No. 1, "St. John's, Mel-rose, No. 1, bis," and the "Lodge of Aberdeen, No. 1, tris." There is evidence of a Lodge at Aberdeen in 1493, of which the present Lodge may well be the direct representative; but the earliest actual minutes that are known are those of the Lodge of Edinburgh, Mary Chapel. Operative Masonry, it ought to be added, persisted longer in Scotland than in England, and the Lodges were more largely operative as to membership—though there were some speculative members from very early times, to go no further back than 1600.

No doubt the Masons of Scotland were well aware of what went on in London in 1717-1721, but they were slow to act, perhaps because the Lodges in the land of heather and cakes were much more closely associated with the trade of building than were those in England.

Such a movement, in which the loosely knit Craft was forming into a Fraternity, was not to be ignored even by conservative craft-Masons. There is evidence, too, that certain members of the Grand Lodge of London attempted to enlist the interest of their Brethren in Scotland in the new Masonry. Anyway, we read of a conference that Desaguliers held with the Lodge of Edinburgh (Mary Chapel) in 1721, when he, though a Speculative, was able to prove himself a Mason to the satisfaction of the Brethren. Scottish Masonry may also have influenced the Grand Lodge of London, through Anderson and others, as for example in the use of the compound words Entered-Apprentice and Fellow-Craft, terms hitherto unknown in England. Nor can we believe that it was merely a coincidence that so many English Grand Masters were Scottish noblemen.

None the less, it was not until 1735 that any move was made in Scotland looking toward the forming of a Grand Lodge. There is a minute of Canongate Kilwinning Lodge, No. 2, telling that a committee was appointed for the purpose of "framing proposals to be laid before the several Lodges, in order to the choosing of a Grand Master for Scotland." Within a year —September 20th, 1736—the Canongate Lodge was visited by a deputation from Kilwinning Scots Arms in regard to the subject, and a month later the Lodge instructed its representatives to bring the matter properly before the four Lodges in and near Edinburgh. The committee acted at once, and the invitation seems to have been extended not only to the Lodges in or near

Edinburgh, but to Lodges all over Scotland. Meantime, a difficulty had been removed. Two old documents known as the St. Clair Charters, of dates 1602 and 1628, conferred the position of hereditary Patron and Judge of the Craft for a particular area on the St. Clair family. But in May, 1736, William St. Clair, the only representative of the family was initiated into Masonry in the Canongate Lodge, and voluntarily renounced his "right, claim and pretence" to the hereditary office. While it is extremely doubtful if he had anything to renounce, as the ancient authority had to do only with Operative Masonry, the disinterested spirit of his "abdication" and his zeal for the good of the Craft, won him the first Grand Mastership in the Assembly soon after convoked.

Over one hundred Lodges had been invited to send representatives to the first General Assembly. Of that number but thirty-three attended, and to avoid jealousy they were placed on the roll in the order in which they entered the Hall: Mary's Chapel first, Kilwinning second. Some Lodges in the country and even in Edinburgh still considered they might join the Grand Lodge or continue independent, at their pleasure, and this, from time to time, made friction. The Mother Kilwinning Lodge, as it was called, seceded because it was placed second on the roll, and remained independent until 1807. St. John's Lodge, Melrose, never joined until 1891. In 1808 certain members of Lodge Caledonia, Maty's Chapel, and other Edinburgh Lodges were expelled on account of political matters. Whereupon they organized a body called "Associated Lodges seceding from the present Grand Lodge of Scotland," and appointed a Grand Master. The dispute was dragged into the courts, which decided in favor of the "Associated Lodges," but everything was cleared up in 1813. Haughfoot Lodge never resigned its independence, and the Lodge of Melrose still declines to recognize any authority superior to its own inherent right of rule.

There has never been any question of conflict or interference between the Grand Lodges of England and Scotland, the later body maintaining cordial relations with both the rival Grand Lodges during the Great Schism. By the time the Grand Lodge of Scotland was organized the ceremonies and system of degrees was very like those in use in England, with certain additions derived from customs and laws peculiar to Scotland. Each Grand body grew in influence and power, spreading over the whole earth, with Lodges in remote lands that sprung from one or the other of them. Second only to the Grand Lodge of England as to numbers, and second to none in the antiquity of its Lodges, the history of the Grand Lodge of Scotland is an honor and a glory to the Craft. Its Constitutions were revised in 1829. In 1872 it recognized the Past Master ceremonial of Installation, making valid the ritual of Installed Master as used in England. It is hardly necessary to add that what is called the Scottish Rite has no connection with Scotland.

IV

In point of date the Grand Lodge of Ireland is second in seniority only to that of England, and followed it at a close interval. There was no native Masonry in Ireland, so far as we have record. Its Cathedrals seem to have been built by Lodges of English Masons, who returned when they had finished their labors. Yet Masonry was not altogether unknown, by hearsay at least, in Ireland, if we may judge from some satirical phrases in under-graduate University songs, as far back as 1688. One song of that date speaks of "being free-masonized in the new way," whatever that may have meant. Later, in 1712, so the story goes, there was a Lodge in Ireland, at which Miss St. Leger—afterwards the Hon. Mrs. Aldworth— was caught eaves-dropping, and was thereupon made a Mason. There must have been some kind of Masonic activity in Dublin, as well as Cork and elsewhere, but no record of it has come down to us.

Nor do we know the early history of the Grand Lodge of Ireland, except that in 1725 we find it already at work—a fact which we owe to the researches of Crawley. In speaking of the election of the Earl of Rosse Grand Master Crawley remarks, that "the terms in which the ceremony is described leave little room for doubt that the Grand Lodge was no sudden creation, but had been then in existence long enough to develop a complete organization of Grand Officers, with subordinate Lodges." The Grand Lodge of Munster appears fully organized in 1726, but where or when it was established we do not know. Indeed we know of only three Lodges under its obedience, the "First Lodge of Ireland, Cork," and Lodges at Waterford and Clonmel: it came to an end in 1733, since which time the Grand Lodge of Dublin has been the governing body of the Craft. A book of Constitutions was published in 1730, little more than a reprint of the Anderson Constitutions of 1723, with items added down to date, but with no further account of its own early history.

To the diligence of Crawley, the antiquary and scholar, we are indebted for the earliest reference to the Royal Arch. It was found in an account of the proceedings of a Lodge at Younghall in 1743. The record says that the members walked in procession, and preceding the Master was "The Royal Arch carried by two Excellent Masons." The next notice of the Degree is found in a pamphlet entitled *Serious and Impartial Enquiry into the cause of the present Decay of Free-Masonry in the Kingdom of Ireland*, by Dr. Dassigny, printed and bound up with the General Regulations of the Grand Lodge in 1741. He speaks of an Assembly of Royal Arch Masons at York, from which city, he says, it was introduced into Dublin; and that it was "an organized body of men who have passed the chair."

So much for a sketch, brief and imperfect—hardly more than a skeleton—of Modern Masonry in the British Isles. Much as we should like to linger over many details and personalities—as, for example, the ambulatory warrants granted to Lodges in the regiments accompanying the Army on tours of service, taking

Masonry to India and America—we must pass along another path, following the Craft to the continent of Europe, where it took strange forms and endured untoward vicissitude.

CHAPTER VI—THE OLD WORLD

AS soon as our gentle Craft crossed the English Channel to the Continent it found itself in a new environment and atmosphere, very unlike anything it had known in its native land. Both politically and ecclesiastically the climate was different and change was inevitable, due as much to tendencies within as to antagonism without. Gould quotes a writer of 1798 as saying that the simple Freemasonry imported from England had been totally changed in every country in Europe, either by the imposing ascendency of French Brethren, or by the injection of doctrines and ceremonies and ornaments of the Parisian Lodges. Truly, if Masonry be changed as to its doctrines, ceremonies and ornaments, not much is left of the original.

The circumstances surrounding the introduction of Masonry into Europe held promise of its perversion— to use a plain word kindly—to uses alien to its original spirit and purpose. Founded, for the most part, by political exiles from England, it was marked at the outset as a secret political society, and that taint, too often justified by facts, has followed its history. Added to this disaster, the tendency within the Craft to the most fertile and fantastic over-elaboration of ceremony, by adding all kinds of "higher degrees," made up of fictions, fancies and every sort of occult absurdity, has often so obscured the simple principles and purposes of the Fraternity that at times, and for long periods, everything resembling Masonry as we know it seemed to vanish entirely into a cloud of confused and many-colored phantasmagoria—a gorgeous panorama as unlike our Craft Masonry as a bird of paradise is unlike a skylark.

There is the further fact, never to be forgotten, of the enmity and antagonism of the Latin Church, now open, now insidious, but always insistent and implacable, making a situation so difficult and dangerous, and so alien to anything we have known in Protestant countries—except during the Morgan episode in America—that we are ill-fitted to understand, much less to pass judgment, in matters so foreign to our own experience. All these facts and forces must be kept in mind as we follow, even in a meager sketch, the fortunes of Masonry in Europe, if we are to be fair to our Brethren, as surely we must be, however widely we may differ from their point of view, or however deeply we may regret some of their decisions. It is very easy to discount the force of temptations we have not felt and to underestimate an opposition the constant impact of which we have not known.

I

Taking France first, we discover a diversity of opinion among our historians as to the exact date when Masonry made its advent. Some place it as early as 1721, others as late as 1732, but it is probable that there was a Lodge at Dunkirk at the earlier date. If we may believe Lalande, the astronomer, whose *Franche-Ma-connerie* appeared in 1773, the first Lodge in France was founded by British Jacobites—fellows of the mad Duke of Whorton and partisans of the Pretender—in 1725. It was called Lodge St. Thomas, in honor of the patron saint of architecture, and apparently worked under the authority of the Grand Lodge of England, but it conducted its affairs secretly until 1736, which may be the reason why the later date is given as the date of its founding. By 1736 there seems to have been some sort of Grand Lodge, as Gould quotes a German authority to the effect that in 1736 the Earl of Darwentwater was chosen to succeed James Hector Maclean, a previous Grand Master.

No opposition was encountered by the Craft in France until 1737, when it was handled rather arbitrarily in Paris by Herault, the Lieutenant of Police. Nor did the Papal Bull launched the following year have any bad effect, except to expose the Craft to public ridicule in the journals and on the stage. At a great Masonic festival held in June, 1738, at Luneville, the Earl of Darwentwater resigned as Grand Master, and was followed by Duc d'Antin, under whose reign the Craft was flooded by a profusion of so-called "Scots degrees," founded upon the fiction·that Scottish crusaders—sword in one hand and trowel in the other —discovered a lost and sacred word in the vault of the Temple at Jerusalem, and that after the suppression of the Templars and the execution of their last historical Grand Master, his alleged successor, Pierre d'Aumont, with seven other knights, fled to Scotland, and there preserved the occult wisdom of the world. For certain reasons, also, those fugitive knights were said to have joined the Guilds of Masons in Scotland, and thus to have given rise to the Society of Freemasons—a "likely" tale, indeed, but good enough to serve as the airy basis of "higher degrees" which made Masonry a thing of form and show.

Duc d'Antin died in 1743, and four days later Prince Louis de Bourbon was elected Grand Master. On the same day the first French Code of Masonic Laws was published, and the Grand Lodge took the title of Grande Loge Anglaise de France. Prince Louis reigned until his death in 1771, amid a riotious luxuriance of "higher" degrees, making a schism resulting in the formation of a Sovereign Council in 1762. Out of this muddle came an attempt to amalgamate the "High Degrees" with the Grand Lodge, and in March, 1773, the Grand Loge Nationale was set up, which later in the same year became known as the Grand Orient de France. A Commission was appointed to report on "Higher Degrees," and the Lodges were directed to work, meantime, in the three symbolical degrees only. By 1784 the Grand Orient had reduced the multitude of "degrees" to four, thereby investing with its authority the *Rite Moderne,* in accordance with which most of the French Lodges work today.

Alas, in 1793 the red whirlwind of Revolution well nigh obliterated the Craft. The Grand Master, Duc d'Orleans, was guillotined, and most of the Lodges were closed. After the storm of blood and terror, not as Grand Master, but as Grand Venerable, Roettiers de Montaleau, gathered up the remnants and constructed a new Grand Orient in 1795, under police sanction, with which what was left of the old Grand Lodge of France was united in 1796, making the present Grand Orient. Later Napoleon agreed that his brother Joseph should be Grand Master—though he was not a Mason at the time, and had to be initiated—and a brilliant epoch of Masonry followed. There was some political disturbance in 1814 and the office of Grand Master was abolished, three Grand Conservators being chosen to discharge the duties. When Napoleon returned from Elba the Grand Master was reinstated, only to be deposed after Waterloo.

Again there was a war of Rites, interrupted by the political events of 1848, which led to bitter attacks upon the Craft in which the clerical party took an active part. Two Grand Masters—Prince Lucien and Marshal Magnan—ruled between 1852 and 1871, when the office was abolished, and the Grand Orient has since been ruled by a President de l'Ordre. Beginning with 1878 there was a general withdrawal of recognition of the Grand Orient of France, led by the Grand Lodge of England, one charge being that it had become agnostic in its teaching and no longer required the Bible to be displayed in its Lodges. What it really did was to strike from its Constitutions an affirmation of belief in Deity. As a matter of fact, from its foundation till 1849, the Constitution of the Grand Orient contained no declaration of belief in Deity, yet during all those years it was fully recognized by the Masonic world. In August, 1849, the following clause was inserted in the Constitution: "Freemasonry has for its principles the existence of Deity and the immortality of the soul."

As this declaration brought the Grand Orient into direct conflict with the Church—on the ground, as the clerical party affirmed, that it was setting up a rival religion—in September, 1877, the following words were substituted: "Masonry has for its principles mutual tolerance, respect for others and for itself, and absolute liberty of conscience." For making this change the Grand Orient was disfellowshipped by nearly every Grand Lodge in the world, especially in English-speaking lands; whereas it was only a return to its original position, when, as has been said, it was regarded as truly Masonic. The change was proposed, not by an atheist—if there be such a thing outside an insane asylum—but by Brother Desmons, a Protestant Christian minister, the object being to parry the criticism that Masonry was trying to foster a spurious religion. At the same time it was left optional with the Lodges to display or not to display the Bible in their ceremonies.

Whether or not such action was wise, or even necessary, is not to be discussed here: it is enough to state the facts and reasons. During the World-War—a few before that time—some American Grand Lodges revised their attitude toward the Grand Orient of France, and extended it recognition as a Masonic body. Others still hold aloof. The Grand Lodge of England stood firm, though the two countries were Allies in a desperate struggle; and in 1914 a Regular and Independent Grand Lodge of France and the Colonies was established in Paris, and recognized by the Grand Lodge of England and other bodies. It works on the lines of English Masonry, using the Rectified Rite of Switzerland. However, it is a small body, with perhaps a dozen Lodges, if so many, and makes headway slowly in a land which has its own Masonry, and will no doubt keep it. Everyone must regret that such an unfortunate tangle should have made France less influential Masonically than it has a right to be, while it also robs Masonry of the universality to which, by virtue of its principles, it has a rightful claim.

II

No English Lodges seem to have been set up in Belgium until 1765, when we find one at Alost, another at Ghent in 1768, another at Mons in 1770. Under Joseph II., in what was then the Austrian Netherlands, the Craft grew and flourished, but in 1786 all but three Lodges were closed; and the following year the edict was made absolute. Yet Masonry, a secret Order, knows how to live in secret. Until 1814 Belgium Masonry lived under the eaves, so to speak, of the Grand Orient of France. Then, for a brief time, the Belgium and Dutch Lodges lived in union, until 1830, when Belgium obtained its Masonic, as well as its political, independence.   Three years later the Grand Orient **of** Belgium was established, and still flourishes.

By virtue of a special Deputation by Lord Lovel, Grand Master of England, the Earl of Chesterfield called an emergent Lodge at the Hague, in Holland, over which Desaguliers presided—as impressive in conferring degrees as he was in helping to fashion them —for the purpose of initiating the Duke of Lorraine, afterwards Emperor Francis I., who subsequently received the Third Degree in England.   So Masonry began in Dutchland, a permanent Lodge in 1735, a Grand Lodge in 1756 with fourteen Lodges, some of English and some of Scotch origin.   When Holland came under French rule the Grand Orient tried to establish itself in that province, but to no avail.   Prince Frederick William, son of King William I., was elected Grand Master of Holland in 1816, and remained at the head of the Dutch Craft until his death in 1881.   The Grand Orient of the Netherlands is not a large body, but both able and active, with Lodges in South Africa and the Dutch Colonies.

The Swedish Rite need not detain us, because it is hardly in the tradition we are here tracing, being an odd mixture of English Masonry, of the so-called "Scots" degrees, with bits of the French Rite and Templarism, joined with certain ideas of Rosicrucian origin, with touches of the mystical teachings of Swedenborg, the great seer of Sweden: a skein too tangled to unravel—dating, it may be added, from 1735.   In Denmark there seems to have been an English Provincial Grand Lodge as early as 1749, and a Scottish body of a sort similar in 1753, Masonry having entered the Danish lands by way of Berlin: but Gould tells us that in 1765 that Danish Craft went over to what is called the Strict Observance—a fantastic creation of alleged Scottish ancestry, concocted by the makers of pseudo-higher degrees—and so wandered out of our orbit; albeit very beautiful and impressive, it is said, and as effective as it was picturesque.

In the dominions of the now vanished Czar Masonry dated from 1732, when James Keith, a soldier of fortune in the Russian service, became Master of a Lodge in St. Petersburg. An English patent as Provincial Grand Master was granted him in 1740. For a time the Craft grew, patronized by the nobility, with the Emperor as acting Master. Other forms of Masonry found footing, including the Strict Observance and the Swedish Rite, as well as a native Masonry led by Count Melisino. In 1772 General Yelaguin was appointed Provincial Grand Master under England, and Lodges rapidly increased. However, in 1774, Yelaguin and the Lodges under him shifted to the Swedish Rite. Keen opposition to the Craft developed, and open meetings had to be given up. Even so, from 1808 to 1822 the Craft prospered, until in that year Alexander, like a bolt out of a blue sky, issued an edict closing all Lodges. Its effect was paralyzing, and since then there has been no Masonry to speak of in Russia. There is, however, a Grand Lodge in the Ukraine, founded in 1900, but not proclaimed until 1919.

III

Of German Masonry we find a first trace—albeit faint—in the appointment of Fredericus du Thom as Provincial Grand Master for the circle of Lower Saxony by the Duke of Norfolk in 1730. Yet du Thom remains a filmy figure in German Masonry, if indeed he is known at all. Three years later the Earl of Strathmore is said to have granted to "eleven German Masons, good brothers," a deputation to open a Lodge in Hamburg, but no trace of such a Lodge has been found. Apparently the first Lodge actually set up in Germany at Hamburg in 1737, under Charles Sarry, had no English warrant, so far as we are aware. Howbeit, three years later its Master had it registered under the English obedience, and was himself appointed a Provincial Grand Master. This oldest of German Lodges had the honor of initiating, in 1738, the Crown Prince of Prussia—later Frederick the Great —who became a devotee of the Craft, setting up a private Lodge in his castle of Rheinsberg. The royal private Lodge ceased when the King went to the first Silesian War, but he gave permission for another to be erected in Berlin in 1740, out of which grew the oldest of the Prussian Grand Lodges—the Three Globes in Berlin.

There is no need to recite in detail the story of the eight Grand Lodges in Germany, or the tale of the five Independent Lodges, because not all of them sprang from, or remained loyal to, the Grand Lodge of England. With the advent of the Rite of Strict

Observance, to which reference has been made, a great confusion—one might call it a plague—fell upon German Masonry, and upon all northern Europe. Even the oldest Grand Body, The Grand National Mother Lodge of the Three Globes, to give its full name, had meant to yield to the strict Observance, on condition that it be given the place of honor; and, failing that prize, declared itself independent. It adopted a system of seven degrees which, with a few later alterations, is still in force.

Note must be made of the Grand Lodge of Prussia in Berlin, founded in 1760, and after July, 1765, called Royal York of Friendship, because Edward, Duke of York—brother of King George III.—was initiated in it. The Lodge then obtained a Warrant of Constitution from England, severing its connection with the Three Globes, and remained true to its allegiance through all the wars of Rites. It grew, founded other Lodges, and became a Grand Lodge in 1798. For the rest, in 1773 Zinnendorf, founder of the National Grand Lodge in Berlin, made a compact with the Grand Lodge of England, by which all Germany was handed over to that Body, using the Swedish Rite—Frankfort-on-the-Main alone dissenting, on the ground that it wished to remain under the English obedience. This led to a rupture with the Grand Lodge of England when, by the terms of the compact, the Grand Master of England declined to renew the patent making the Frankfort Lodge a Provincial Grand Lodge. Evidently the Grand Lodge of England took this fashion of fighting the Rite of Strict Observance—preferring the Swedish Rite instead, if its own were rejected—but it did allow the old Lodge of Hamburg, which became a Grand Lodge, to adopt the Strict Observance and yet remain, in some degree, under English rule.

Masonry in Germany, of whatever Rite, has always flourished, being both highly influential and richly benevolent; but it is a little difficult to determine what the conditions are today, after the Great War. The old Grand Lodges and Unions of Grand Lodges remain, to which has been added the new Grand Lodge of the Rising Sun at Nurnburg—a pacifist body not yet recognized, and not to be confused with the old Grand Lodge of the Sun at Bayreuth. So far as one can discover the facts, there seems to be a new alignment in German Masonry: on the one side the old Prussian Grand Lodges—ultra-conservative, ardently Christian, and intensely nationalistic, if such words be not utterly contradictory; and another group of Grand Lodges enthusiastically humanitarian and international in their outlook. Plainly the first group tolerate the Republic but hate it, while the second is trying to interest the new Germany in the Craft.

A recent letter has this paragraph:—"The 9th of November, 1918, and the events following it—meaning the rise of the Republic—were and have been a surprise not only to the German nation, but also to its Freemasonry. The Craft, as such, had nothing to do with the establishment of the Republic which followed the downfall of the monarchy. Nor did the disciples of the Royal Art follow the example of the nation in democratizing the form of the Masonic establishment, but retained the more or less oligarchical character of their Grand Lodges. Yet, in keeping with the Constitution of Masonry—which prescribes that we support the constituted government of the land, that we 'give no umbrage or ground of political jealousy to the government for the time being'—the Lodges cheerfully abide by and support the new government."

IV

Masonry in Austria-Hungary has had a troubled history, as might have been expected. A Lodge was set up in Prague by Count Sporck, on returning from his travels, as early at 1729, from which other Lodges grew in Galicia, Hungary, Styria, and Moravia. But the first Lodge erected in Vienna, in 1742, was quicky closed by Maria Theresa, though her Consort, Francis of Lorraine, belonged to it. By his influence it enjoyed intermittent toleration, in secret, and had passed under the Strict Observance by the time Theresa died in 1780. In Hungary a Lodge is known to have existed in 1766, and eight other Lodges shortly afterward; the first at Pressburg, but under what Rite we do not know. The Craft took new life in Vienna under Joseph II, and by 1784 there was a Grand Lodge ruling over forty-five Lodges, but it lived only a year and was swept away by imperial Edict. With fitful revivals form time to time, after the Great War, in 1918, a Grand Lodge was formed in Vienna; but in Hungary the Craft is interdicted.

In Italy, as in all Latin lands, Masonry has had an uncertain and precarious tenure, though a Lodge was founded at Florence by Lord George Sackville as far back as 1733. By 1735 Lodges were reported at Milan, Verona, Padua, Vicenza, Venice and Naples, but in 1738 the Vatican launched its thunders against the Craft with deadly effect. For a brief time, under French rule, the Order grew; when Napoleon fell it was well nigh obliterated. However, it reappeared in 1859, and in the days of Garibaldi it had no small part in the making of a free and united Italy. A Grand Orient was formed at Turin in 1862, which eleven years later merged with the Scottish Rite. A new Grand Orient founded at Milan in 1901 today has its seat in Rome. As we write Signor Mussolini is again trying to suppress Italian Masonry, and naturally so, because the Craft do not accept his dictum that "Men are tired of liberty."

Under the authority of the Grand Lodge of England a Provincial Grand Lodge was erected in Geneva, Switzerland, in 1737. A year later, and often afterward, the magistrates issued orders to suppress all Lodges, but the Craft, so far from obeying, made vigorous replies in the press. The Rite of Strict Observance had its demoralizing effect in Switzerland, as everywhere else in Europe. Also, the Grand Orient of France sought to capture the country, but seven Genevan Lodges, remaining faithful to the English system, organized a Grand Orient of Geneva, in 1789, under English rule. After various vicissitudes and a mingling of Rites—including the French, the Helvetic and the Scots Directory,—a general union was effected in 1844, resulting in the present Grand Lodge Alpina. Swiss Masons have been leaders in the advocacy of Masonic universality, of which we hear so much and do not see enough.

After all, Masonry must have in it something which holds men by a tie strangely strong, else they would not dare and suffer so much in its behalf. Surely in no country on earth has our kindly Craft had so tormented a career as in Spain, where a Lodge was set up in Madrid in 1728 by the exiled Duke of Whorton; and another the same year at Gibraltar. Alas, in 1740, as a result of the Papal Bull, Philip V issued an edict by which the members of the Lodge of Madrid were either thrown into prison or sent to the galleys. Ten years later Ferdinand VII condemned Masons to death without trial or mercy; in 1793 the Cardinal Vicar repeated the decree. Meantime, all the infernal machinery of the Inquisition was used against the Craft, but it lived none the less. Under Joseph Napoleon there was respite, and Masonry prospered, forming a National Grand Lodge. With his downfall the Inquisition returned, and perilous times followed. As to the state of affairs today it is hard to find out, except that the Grand Orient was dissolved in 1922.

Such is the story—repeated in Portugal—of Latin Masonry; a story of brave beginnings, savage persecutions, incredible endurance, and desperate loyalty. But enough: we cannot here follow Masonry into

Greece, Bulgaria, Turkey, Roumania, much less into Asia Minor, India, and the Far East and the Isles of the Sea, where it has journeyed, a dim light in beshadowed lands, a witness for liberty in the darkness of despotism, a prophet of simple faith in the night of superstition.   It is time to turn our eyes westward from the Old World to the New, where Masonry has had its greatest development, and where, if it be worthy of its heroic past, it will have a future to which no man can set a limit.

CHAPTER VII—THE NEW WORLD

I

WHEN, where, and by whom did Masonry make its advent into the New World, in whose liberal air it has grown to be so great? Nobody knows, nor is it our present concern to enquire, if by Masonry is meant the few vague hints left us. A slab of trap rock discovered in Nova Scotia with the date 1606 and what some thought to be the Square and Compasses deeply cut in it, though much worn by time and weather; the rumor of a group of Hebrews at Newport, Rhode Island, in 1656, who gave one of their number "the degrees of Masonrie"; the story that in 1670 there came to John Eliot, the Apostle to the Indians, from England, a box of books with Masonic emblems, to be forwarded to South Carolina— these are myths, manifestly apocryphal, and are worth what they are worth, but offer nothing in the shape of facts.

The Pilgrims and the Puritans were not of our Craft, and if we may judge from their real interests we may be sure that they did not care anything about it. Nor is it likely that there were many Masons, if any, Operative or Speculative, to be found among the earliest immigrants to America. Later we find intimations, if nothing more, of Masons on this side of the Atlantic, among civil or military officers, if we may believe the story, which some of us do not, of John Moore, Collector of the Port of Philadelphia, who, in a letter said to have been written in 1715, spoke of having "spent a few evenings in festivity with my Masonic Brethren." Such gatherings, if they were held, were hardly to be described as Lodges, but informal meetings having no officers with terms which outran each closing, and leaving no records. Of course, if any such group, or groups, did meet as Lodges they were regular, but not duly constituted in our sense of the word.

Further back we hear of Americans who were made Masons in England, as for example Jonathan Belcher, afterward Governor of Massachusetts and New Hampshire, who was made a Mason in England in 1704, presumably in London; and he has the honor of being the first American Mason. Indeed, if we may take as a token the number of news items of a Masonic sort in the early press, especially in Boston—sometimes veiled, sometimes open—there must have been a sufficient number of Masons to justify such items, or else a very lively interest in the subject about the time the Grand Lodge of England was organized. For example, the *Boston News Letter*, for Jan. 5th, 1718, under the head of news for the Port of Boston, says; "Outward Bound, Jacob William Ship Charles and Freemason for Jamaica." Other items regarding the same ship appear in later issues. Certain hints seem to point to the fact that a Lodge of Masons met, for a brief time, in King's Chapel in Boston; but the story neither rises to the grade of proof nor falls to the level of tradition. Andrew Belcher, son of the Governor, was made a Mason on this side of the Atlantic some time prior to 1733, as were at least ten others who in that year applied to Henry Price for the Constitution of the first Lodge "made here"; but no one knows when, where or how they were made Masons.

Which brings us to the kind of Masonry dealt with in this sketch, that is the Masonry derived from and sanctioned by the Grand Lodge of England, and within these limits our task is not so difficult. Happily it has been made easier by a recent book of great interest and value, entitled *The Beginnings of Freemasonry in America*, by Melvin M. Johnson, a critical and competent study of facts and sources, at once an honor to its author and a permanent treasure to the Craft. There we find a reference to all that is now known of Masonry in the New World prior to 1750, and its arrangement in chronological order makes it a kind of diary of the advent and evolution of Masonry in America. It was written, the author tells us, because in the New World, as in the Old, the fathers of Masonry were careless of records, so much so that the first Provincial Grand Lodge, like the Mother Grand Lodge, has no formal record of events until long after the time of their happening—not until 1750.

II

As we have noted in an earlier chapter, in June, 1730, the Duke of Norfolk, Grand Master of England, appointed Daniel Coxe, Esq, of New Jersey, the first Provincial Grand Master in the New World, his jurisdiction to include New York, New Jersey, and Pennsylvania, his deputation authoritative for two years. But Coxe, as all now agree, did not exercise his deputation, and was not in America at all until after its authority had expired—nor is there any evidence that it was ever renewed.   Instead, he remained in England trying to perfect his title to a vast area of North America, to which he laid claim by virtue of a grant to his father, who was physician to Charles I and II. On Jan. 29, 1731, he was present at a meeting of the Grand Lodge of England, and during the year he was registered as a member of Lodge No. 8, meeting at the Devil Tavern within Temple Bar.   No indication has been found of his presence in America until 1734, by which time his commission has expired, and he seems to have lost interest in Masonic affairs.

During the year 1730 we find in the *Pennsylvania Gazette*, of which Benjamin Franklin was editor, a number of items of news about Masonry—one of them an account of the meeting of the Grand Lodge in London—which shows that the editor, though not a member of the Craft, deemed the items of interest.   In December he published in the *Gazette* an alleged exposé of Masonry which had been for a time circulated in England, with the remark: "As there are several Lodges of Free-Masons erected in this Province, we think the following will not be unacceptable to our readers."   Whether there were "several" Lodges is doubtful, but there was one—not, technically, a regular Lodge in the sense that it was recognized by the Grand

Lodge of England, but working by inherent right—in which Franklin himself was initiated the following Febrary, 1731, "according to the old Customs." This Lodge met first as a private, and, later, as a Grand Lodge, of which Franklin was Master and Grand Master in 1734.

Meantime, on April 13th, 1733, under the Grand Mastership of Lord Montague, a Deputation was issued to Henry Price as "Provincial Grand Master of New England and the Dominions and Territories thereunto belonging"; by virtue of which Price became the father and founder of regular Masonry in the New World. On July 30th, following, Price formed a Grand Lodge in Boston, appointing Andrew Belcher his Deputy Grand Master, and Thomas Kennelly and John Quane, Grand Wardens. He then caused his Deputation to be read, after which he received a petition of eighteen Brethren addressed to him, praying that they might be constituted into a regular Lodge by virtue of his Deputation. The petition was granted, and the first Lodge held under written authority in America was formed at the Bunch of Grapes Tavern, King Street, Boston, Aug. 31st, 1733. The original petition, in the handwriting of Henry Hope, who was chosen Master, is still in the archives of the Grand Lodge of Massachusetts.

Later in the year Franklin visited Boston and met Henry Price, Provincial Grand Master, from whom he no doubt received the copy of the Constitutions of 1723, which he reprinted in Philadelphia the following year—the first Masonic book printed in America. In

1734 Franklin wrote to Price, "whose authority and power," he understood, "had been extended over all America"—as it had been in August of that year— asking him to confirm the Brethren of Philadelphia in the privilege of holding a Grand Lodge annually in their customary manner. The request was not only granted, but Franklin was appointed Provincial Grand Master of Pennsylvania, under Price, now "Grand Master of His Majesty's Dominions in North America," Feb. 21st, 1734: which shows that Gould was in error when he said that the Philadelphia Lodge "never, until 1749, worked under any sanction which was deemed superior to its own."

In point of priority, then, the following Lodges have precedence in the history of regularly constituted Lodges in America: the Lodge of Boston in 1733; the Lodge at Montserrat second, in 1734; the Lodge of Philadelphia in 1734-5; the Lodge in Savannah, Georgia, and the Lodge in Charleston, South Carolina, in 1735; the Lodge in Portsmouth, New Hampshire, in 1736; and so on as the list lengthened. The earliest American By-Laws or Regulations of a Lodge were adopted in 1733, but no mention is made of any degrees. Masons were either "made" or "admitted," and nothing more until 1736, when for the first time the degree of Fellow-Craft is named. Not until three years later, however, do we find such an entry as the following, in Portsmouth, New Hampshire: "Capt. Andrew Tombes was made a Mason and *raised* to a Fellow-Craft." The records of Tun Tavern Lodge, of

Philadelphia, in 1849, use the words "entered," "passed" and "raised" as we use them now. Johnson adds:

"Those who are familiar with the history of the ritual and its development in England, Ireland and Scotland, will at once, I think, conclude rightly that the first degree, in these early days in America, contained what has now been expanded into the first and second; also that the second degree corresponds to what is now the third. But few Brethren advanced beyond Entered Apprentices, upon which degree all general business was transacted. But what shall we say when we find a Masters' Lodge constituted December 22, 1738? Before then the only references to Masters were to the Masters of Lodges. . . . At the next monthly meeting, with ten present and Henry Price in the chair, George Monerieff was 'raised a Master.' . . . What then was the Masters' Degree? Again we must appeal to the ritualistic history of Freemasonry in the British Isles. I believe the answer to be that the degree worked by the Masters' Lodge was what is sometimes known as the Chair Degree or installation of a Master, absorbed nowadays in the United States by the Royal Arch Chapter and transformed into the degree of Past Master."

III

So much for the beginnings; we must now quicken our pace through a maze of facts and events, in the effort to give a large outline of American Masonic history. On the death of Tomlinson, who succeeded

Price as Provincial Grand Master of New England, in 1737, Thomas Oxnard—an initiate of the first Lodge of Boston—received that honor in 1743. At his death in 1754, a petition asking that Jeremy Gridley be made his successor closes with the statement that since 1733 Lodges in Philadelphia, New Hampshire, South Carolina, Antigua, Nova Scotia, Newfoundland, Rhode Island, Maryland, and Connecticut, "have received Constitutions from us"—assuredly a notable record of good work well done. By the terms of his patent—received in 1755—the authority of Gridley was restricted to those parts of North America for which no Provincial Grand Master had been named.

The Great Schism in England, in 1751, the story of which has been told in brief, was very quickly reflected in the Colonial Lodges. The "Ancients," as a matter of fact, soon became predominant in the New World, and we may be glad that it was so, otherwise the story of Masonry in the Revolution, as we shall see, might have been very different. This triumph was due to the indefatigable industry of Dermott as a propagandist, and hardly less to the clever use which he made of his affiliations with the Grand Lodge of Scotland. Indeed, he introduced his system into New England largely, if not entirely, through his alliance with Scotland. In 1760 a self-constituted Lodge—St. Andrew's —to which so many famous men of the city afterward belonged—received a Scottish warrant, *granted* four years before. Later, in 1767, when Provincial Grand Master Gridley died—succeeded by John Rowe—steps

were taken at once to form a rival Provincial Grand
Lodge under the Scottish obedience.   A petition to that
effect was signed by the officers of St. Andrew's Lodge,
joined by three military Lodges attached to the British
Army, all four using the "Ancient" system.   The petition was granted, and Joseph Warren was appointed
Grand Master of Masons in Boston, and within a
hundred miles of the city.

That is to say, St. Andrew's Lodge became a Provincial Grand Lodge, as the association of the military
Lodges was only nominal.   In 1769 a group of St.
Andrew's men, calling themselves a Royal Arch Lodge,
conferred the degree of Knight Templar for the first
time in America, so far as we have documentary record.
Five years later, by a further Scottish patent, Warren
was appointed Grand Master for the Continent of
America, and after his death the body over which he
had presided adopted the title of the Massachusetts
Grand Lodge, its rival, the "Modern" Grand Lodge,
under Rowe, keeping the name of St. John's.   In Pennsylvania the victory of "Ancients" over "Moderns" was
annihilating, so much so that by 1770 all "Modern"
Lodges had ceased to exist, and the "Ancient" Grand
body was setting up Lodges beyond the borders of
Pennsylvania, in other Provinces.

Thus, all along the line, by skill of strategy, by industry, by the adventure of introducing new degrees
—or old ones revamped—the "Ancients" out-generaled
the "Moderns" in the New World, as in the Old.   In
Virginia we find them in control of Port Royal Kil-

winning Cross Lodge—its origin indicated by its name
—and the next year, 1758, they took over the old independent Lodge of Fredericksburg, in which on Nov.
4th, 1752, Washington had been initiated, and where,
under date of 1753, we find "the earliest known minute
referring to the actual working of the Royal Arch
Degree" in America.   Farther down the coast in
Florida the tactics used were still more striking, as
witness the curious history of a Military Lodge, which
became, by turns, "Modern," Scottish, "Ancient," and
finally Scottish once more; a transmigration noted with
peculiar interest by Gould, the historian, who was
Master of that famous Lodge at Gibraltar in 1858.

At this distance, in spite of all the tactics used by the
"Ancients," it is not easy to understand the decline and
defeat of the Mother Grand Lodge in America, in view
of the wise and benign policy of that Grand Lodge in
dealing with Provincial Bodies—a policy unnoted by
nearly every Masonic historian, but which it behooves
us to recall even in this brief narrative, on the eve of
the Revolution.   From the first it had been the policy
of the Grand Lodge not to impose rulers from the
outside upon the Craft in America, but to select only
those who has already been chosen by their Brethren
on this side.   Not only in respect to Grand Masters,
but in the right and privilege of framing their own
domestic laws and rules, the Provincial bodies were
left free and unmolested, provided, of course, the old
landmarks of the Craft were preserved.   If English
statesmen had been as wise in their policy as English

Masons, there would have been no need for a War of Independence, and the separation might have been brought about with as much good feeling politically, as it actually was Masonically.

IV

Indeed, at no time did the Grand Lodge of England ask, much less exact, any tax, levy or subsidy from any Colonial Lodge, and it does not ask it today of the Colonial Lodges that remain under its jurisdiction. Some Grand Lodges, moved by a spirit of goodwill, did remit sums to England for what was known as the Fund of Charity, which was distributed with equal hand to any deserving Mason who applied from either side of the sea; but they were voluntary gifts, gratefully received and faithfully applied. Let us try to imagine what would have been the relation between the Colonies and the English Government, if the same policy had been pursued by statesmen—if, instead of taxing the Colonies to pay debts incurred by England, they had acted after the manner of the Mother Grand Lodge—how different the result might have been.

Unfortunately we cannot here recite in detail the story of Masonry in the Revolution—a thrilling story it is, needing a whole volume to itself—but we ought always to remember that even in those wild and terrible days the Masonic tie was not brother. Fellowship was suspended, but it was not severed, and at the end of the conflict the Craft took up its labors and went forward. As between the "Ancients" and the

"Moderns," it is a curious circumstance, as Gould observes, and deserves to be recorded, that, with notable exceptions, in most of the Provinces the men of the "Ancient" Lodges were ardent supporters of the cause of the Colonists, while the "Modern" Lodges were inclined to side with the Motherland. Here, perhaps, we find the reason why the "Modern" Lodges everywhere declined, and in at least one Province disappeared entirely.

Gould gives, by contrast, a list of the "Modern" Provincial Grand Masters who took the side of England, among them "John Rowe, whose action paralyzed the St. John's Grand Lodge of Boston; William Allen, of Pennsylvania, who attempted to raise a regiment for the British Army; Sir Egerton Leigh, of South Carolina, who, foreseeing the approaching storm, left for England in 1774; and Sir John Johnson of New York, who cast his lot with the Royalists at the commencement of the war." Yet, as has been said, there were notable exceptions, as in the case of New York, where, prior to the war Masonry was a monopoly of the "Moderns," but when the British Army occupied New York City, with it came "Ancient" Masonry, and the formation of a Grand Lodge having nine Lodges, one Scottish, one Irish, and the rest "Ancient." Still, taken as a whole, had it not been for the attitude of the "Ancient" Lodges, the story of Masonry in the Revolution might have been another history, and its position in America today very different from what it is.

What patriotic memories cluster about the old Green Dragon Tavern in Boston, which Webster, speaking at Andover in 1823, called "the headquarters of the Revolution." But he might also have mentioned that it was a Masonic Hall, in the "Long Room" of which St. Andrew's Lodge held its meetings. There Samuel Adams, Paul Revere, Warren, Hancock, Otis and others met, passed resolutions, and then laid schemes to make them come true. There the Boston Tea Party was planned, and executed by Masons disguised as Mohawk Indians—not by the Lodge as such, but by a club formed within the Lodge, calling itself the *Caucus Pro Bono Publico*, of which Warren was the leading spirit, and in which, as Elliott said, "the plans of the Sons of Liberty were matured." As Henry Purkett used to say, he was present at the famous Tea Party as a spectator, and in disobedience to the order of the Master of the Lodge who was actively present: albeit not in his official capacity—just as, later, at the battle of Bunker Hill, though a Major-General of right, he fought and died as a volunteer in the ranks.

As in Massachusetts, so throughout the Colonies, the Masons, especially of the "Ancient" obedience, were everywhere active in behalf of a nation "conceived in liberty and dedicated to the proposition that all men are created equal." Of the men who signed the Declaration of Independence, the following are known to have been members of the order: William Hooper, Benjamin Franklin, Matthew Thornton, William Whipple, John Hancock, Philip Livingston, Thomas Nelson;

and no doubt others, if we had the Masonic records destroyed during the war. Not only Washington, but nearly all his generals were Masons; such at least as Greene, Lee, Marion, Sullivan, Rufus and Israel Putnam, Edwards, Jackson, Gist, Baron Steuben, Baron De Kalb, and the Marquis de Lafayette, who was made a Mason in one of the Military Lodges of the Continental Army, as were Alexander Hamilton and John Marshall. Such facts make one wonder what the Revolution might have been had not its leaders been united by the peculiar tie, at once tender and strong, which Masonry knows how to spin and weave between men in "times that try men's souls."

Another notable exception, in respect of the "Ancient" and "Modern" feud, was the fact that the most famous of the Military Lodges, the "American Union" —a prophetic name—had been chartered by John Rowe, of Boston, the "Modern" Provincial Grand Master, and attached to the "Connecticut line." We have record of a great St. John's Day festival at Morristown, New Jersey, Dec. 27th, 1779, with a large number of members and visitors present,—among them General Washington—when a petition was approved to the several Provincial Grand Masters, to be signed on behalf of the Military Lodges, for the appointment of a Grand Master for the United States of America. Such a convention Lodge, formed of the different lines of the Army, was held in due form under the authority of the American Union Lodge, in Morristown, "the sixth day of March, in the year of

Salvation, 1780." Washington, of course, was naturally named for the office of Grand Master, and it was
hoped that such a united Grand Lodge might heal the
feud between "Moderns" and the "Ancients." The
project, however, fell through and was abandoned.

V

When Warren was killed, Joseph Webb was elected
"Grand Master of Ancient Masonry" in the State of
Massachusetts, the first sovereign and independent
Grand Lodge in America, the second being that of
Virginia set up the following year. Immediately the
war was over and the Treaty of Peace signed, the
Grand Lodge of Pennsylvania constituted itself an
independent body by resolution, which they forwarded
to the Grand Lodge of England in 1783, intimating
that, as the two countries had become separated in
Government, it was thought by Masons that it was
desirable that each of the countries should have their
own separate jurisdiction in Masonry; and therefore
the Grand Lodge of Pennsylvania expressed the wish
that the friendly relations that had existed previously
would always be maintained. Within as brief a time
as possible a reply came back—which is now one of
the most treasured documents in the archives of the
Grand Lodge of Pennsylvania—from the Grand Lodge
of England, heartily accepting the new Constitution,
stating that they agreed with the American Brethren
that in the circumstances, at the close of the conflict, it
was well that sovereign jurisdiction on both sides of

the sea be maintained, and offering the prayer that for all time the friendly relations which had always existed betwen English and American Masonry, and had not been broken, even during civil strife, might remain intact—a piece of history which, as Sir Alfred Robbins said, ought to be known and never forgotten.

Within a few years after the War the feud between the "Ancients" and "Moderns" was healed, a union of rival bodies having been brought about in Boston in 1792, twenty years before the Lodge of Reconciliation in England. In Pennsylvania no "Modern" Lodges were left; in New York both sides fell into line without difficulty; in South Carolina two bodies persisted almost until the Union in England in 1813. Once free, politically as well as Masonically, the Craft in America grew rapidly in influence and power, following the path of the pioneer westward. Down the Atlantic coast, along the Great Lakes, in the wilderness of the Middle West and the forests of the far South, and, finally, over the mountains to the Pacific coast, Masonry set up its altars on the frontiers—symbols of civilization, of loyalty to law and order, of friendship with Home, Church, and State.

For twenty-five years the Craft grew and gained, making quiet but remarkable advance, until, suddenly, without warning, and with the slightest pretex of provocation, it became the victim of the most violent and fanatical persecution, which well nigh swept it away. At this distance it is not easy to understand the attack made upon the Fraternity between 1826 and,

roughly, 1845, in connection with the "Morgan affair," as it was called, due to the fact that one William Morgan, a printer, was kidnapped and carried
off because he was about to expose the secrets of
Masonry, and was never seen again. Admit that a
crime was committed—as it was in all probability, if
we may trust the truest tradition—even so, only mad-
ness could hold a Fraternity responsible for the act
of a few misguided men, especially when the deed was
denounced by Lodges everywhere, and the Governor
of New York, himself a Mason, did all within his
power to detect and punish those involved. Alas, it
was an evil hour; the mob-mind ruled, and the fanati-
cism could not be stayed.

An Anti-Masonic political party was formed, fed by
frenzy, and the land was stirred from end to end.
Even such a man as John Quincy Adams, of great
credulity and strong prejudice, was drawn into the
fray, and in a series of letters flayed Masonry as an
enemy of society and a free State—forgetting that
Washington, Franklin, and Marshall were members of
the Order. Thurlow Weed, Seward, Stevens, and other
politicians of their ilk, were swept into power on the
strength of the fury, as they had planned to do, de-
feating Henry Clay for President, because he was a
Mason—and, incidentally, electing Andrew Jackson,
another Mason. The Anti-Craft party carried only
one state, Vermont, but the Fraternity was almost
shattered. Charters were given up, Lodges closed, and
Masonic work, especially in the northern States, almost

entirely ended. Finally the storm spent itself, leaving the Order purged of feeble men, and the Craft took up its work again.

VI

By the time Masonry had recovered from its ordeal of persecution—its most terrible experience in English-speaking lands—the dark clouds of Civil War hung like a pall over the land. At last the crisis came, dividing a nation one in arts and aims and historic memories, and leaving an entail of blood and fire and tears. Again we have a right to an honorable pride in the fact that, while Churches were severed and States were seceding, the Masonic tie was unbroken in that fateful hour and its black swirl of passions. An effort was made to involve the Craft in the strife, but the wise counsel of leaders, North and South, prevented the mixing of Masonry in politics; and while it could not prevent the tragedy, it did much to mitigate the woe of it. Some day, mayhap, the tale will be told of what Masonry did in those dark years—how it passed through picket lines, eluded sentinels, softened the lot of the prisoner of war, and planted the acacia upon the graves of friends and foes alike.

After the Civil War the nation plunged into a period of stupendous development and prosperity, in which Masonry had its full share, growing with incredible rapidity—as it always does after a war. Lodges multiplied, and every Rite flourished. The care of the aged Brother, his wife, widow, and orphans, enlisted the concern of the Craft. Homes, asylums, hospitals

for the needy and afflicted sprang up everywhere,
Also, about the same time there began a great intel-
lectual advance of the Craft, with the advent of such
men as Pike—master genius of Masonry in America—
Mackey, Parvin, Fort, to name no others, almost
simultaneously with a similar group in England and
Ireland, such as Gould, Hughan, Speth, Crawley, and
others, who founded the famous Quatuor Coronati
Lodge of London, in 1884, dedicated to Masonic re-
search. The result was a more scholarly and authentic
literature of the Craft, replacing the old uncritical
books filled with every kind of fantastic theory of
Masonry and its origin, tracing it back to Noah and
Adam, as if credulity and gullibility were pass-words
of the Lodge. Today there are more than thirty Re-
search Societies in England, and at least one in
America, with the promise of an accurate and more
popular literature within reach and range of the rank
and mass of the Craft.

There is no need to tell of American Masonry as
it now is, except to say that three million Masons,
or thereabouts—more than sixty percent of the Masons
of the world—live and labor in its fifty Grand Lodges.
Meantime it grows almost too fast for assimilation,
and the problems of prosperity are well nigh as difficult as the problems of adversity. The World War
revealed the impotence of Masonry as it is now organized in a manner rather humiliating, at a time
when concerted action was imperatively demanded,
if it was to have any really effective part in the service

of the nation in time of need. The early efforts to form the Craft after the fashion of federal Government failed, and as it has never been united it can hardly be said to be divided: but co-operation was now a necessity. Out of this disconcerting experience was born the Masonic Service Association of the United States, organized in Iowa in 1919, in which more than thirty Grand Lodges have joined hands—making it the greatest co-operative undertaking in the whole history of the Craft. The purpose of the Association is really threefold: Relief in time of national calamity, the Education of Masons in Masonry—its laws, customs, ritual, history, philosophy, and symbolism—and, finally, the Leadership of the Craft in those fields of public service in which the common good can be helped.